The love of possession is a disease with them

The love of

possession is a disease with them

BY TOM HAYDEN

HOLT, RINEHART AND WINSTON

Chicago   New York   San Francisco

Several of the themes in this
book were expressed on the
WNET program, "Free-Time."

Copyright © 1972 by Tom Hayden

Published simultaneously in Canada by Holt, Rinehart
and Winston of Canada, Limited.

Library of Congress Catalog Card Number: 72–77633
ISBN: cloth: 0–03–001301–1
ISBN: paper: 0–03–091989–4
FIRST EDITION

Designer: Betty Binns
PRINTED IN THE UNITED STATES OF AMERICA

To Oanh and Hieu, Chuong and Van, Vy and Lau,
Tien and Hieu, Nguyen Thi Binh and Pham Van Dong

*Yet hear me, people, we have now to deal with another
race—small and feeble when our fathers first met them but
now great and overbearing. Strangely enough they have
a mind to till the soil and the love of possession is a disease
with them. These people have made many rules that the rich
may break but the poor may not. They take their tithes from
the poor and weak to support the rich and those who rule* . . .

—SITTING BULL
at the Powder River Council, 1877

The love of possession is a disease with them

For me the world consisted of several dozen houses
*   built in the center*
of green mountains.

My childhood was in harmony with nature
*   among the gardens, the fields,*
and the mountains.

I was part of my village which I would never leave.

Night and day, in the light of the moon, in the fields,
*   in the forest,*
with the natural music of the birds,
my friends would wander in the most perfect calm,
the happiest in the world.

[3]

We were convinced that in the evil world
there were too few people who were content
with so few things like we were,
and could call it happiness.

When the seasons of planting and sowing came,
together with my friends,
in high spirits,
we fought against every caprice of nature
and thus kept the traditional rhythm of our ancestors.

These are the poetic reflections of a twenty-one-year-old woman from the Plain of Jars, in Laos, who was interviewed in an American-controlled refugee camp. Her once harmonious life had been shattered by American bombs, she had been made a refugee like millions of others in Indochina, and her former homeland (and that of her ancestors) has been turned to wasteland.

Like most people of Indochina, this woman's roots are in an agrarian society of small villages. Their lives have been hard but, as her words beautifully explain, their universe and culture have been whole and satisfying.

The most violent disruption of these ancient cultures has come in the last century with the unwanted expansion of Western power into Asia—mainly the French from the 1860s to 1954, followed by the United States indirectly since 1949 and openly since 1961. Few conflicts could be more total than that between these Asian, predominantly Buddhist, communal rural societies and the competitive materialism and technology of the white West.

Where revolutionary communism has been successful in Indochina, it has arisen not simply as a "modernizing" force, but also in defense of the cultural traditions, the national spirit and accomplishments of these societies. The effect of colonizing powers, on the contrary, has been forcibly to graft alien values on the people under their control.

[4]

After a quarter-century of American military involvement, and although the pressure for American withdrawal has never been greater, peace in Indochina still seems distant. Even if peace came tomorrow, however, this will remain a fact for our conscience to absorb: the Nixon Administration has killed, wounded, displaced, or targeted under fire more people in Indochina than at any time in history, continuing a tradition of Western imperialism which, in America, began with the attempted destruction of the Indian. That is the theme of this book.

My own sense of the historic scope of this conflict has evolved only gradually. In the mid-sixties I knew the escalating war was "somehow" structurally related to the civil rights and poverty crises in America, to our country's war economy and its far-flung system of trade and commerce. The connection then in my mind was: America is racist at home and abroad, and is protecting a status quo empire of property and privilege. These feelings were driven deep into me after two trips to North Vietnam and Cambodia (1965 and 1967) where I experienced US Air Force bombing and then returned to find American cities occupied by troops shooting down black people.

The immediacy, the urgency of these parallels caught me up; I did not yet see the historical dimension of the war. Through 1968 I believed the war could be ended by a crisis in which the conflict would come to a boiling point and the American governing class, being "rational," would decide that its interest was better served by withdrawal than by continued pursuit of control in Vietnam. The year 1968 provided the test: beginning with the extraordinary battle of Tet and ending with the embarrassing spectacle of Chicago, the costs of staying in Vietnam were raised higher than ever.

Like millions of other people I waited to see what the

"New Nixon" government's response would be. That the Nixon Administration, like its predecessor, took these costs of the war quite seriously cannot be doubted. The stated goal of peace, the withdrawals of American troops, the repeated acknowledgment of the unpopularity of the war, all indicated that in fact the government would cut some of the costs of the war.

But the fact that the government has not ended the war itself indicates the seriousness of America's official commitment there from one administration to the next. Though the level and type of violence may change from year to year, one point has not changed since 1949: US determination to prevent the rebel forces of Indochina from coming to power. This American stubbornness suggests that Vietnam is more than a marginal or "limited" conflict, that Vietnam is the defining conflict of our times.

We must face the likelihood that *the United States government, if permitted, will continue its invasion of Indochina for another generation.*

The people of Indochina know this very well because they feel the bombs, they feel the pressures disrupting their lives, no matter what talk of "peace" there is in Washington.

It is the American people who have been deceived—as the Pentagon Papers show—for the past 25 years. Now we are in danger of being deceived again, lied to again, in this coming election year.

The lie is that the war is winding down.

The evidence is that the Vietnam war, rather than ending, is being transformed and continued in a new form. According to the Nixon Doctrine, the Vietnam war under President Johnson was a "mistake" because it relied too heavily on American troops; the general thesis is that America's client states and protectorates, like the Republic of Vietnam, must take greater responsibility for their own defense as America limits its commitments and adopts a "Low Profile." In practice, this doctrine has six main tenets:

(1) The use of massive American firepower and technology instead of American troops.

(2) "Vietnamization": using US-financed and trained native troops against guerrillas, which a highly placed US official calls "changing the color of the corpses."

(3) The forced disruption of people from their traditional lands into refugee camps and urban slums, where they can be better controlled, and the popular basis of guerrilla war (the people) can be destroyed.

(4) The use of economic and political manipulation to sweep the refugees into a Western-oriented commercial economy, part of a "new international division of labor" in the Pacific.

(5) Cultural destruction, the wiping out of the traditional national identity which is the strength both of the Indochinese nations and their anti-American resistance.

(6) A cynicism toward the American people which assumes that we will not care if this is done in our name as long as the casualties are Asian and not American.

Cloaked in phrases about "self-determination," this doctrine posits that people in South Vietnam, for example, would never "freely choose" socialism, and that, indeed, only US intervention affords the conditions for true freedom of choice. The doctrine is an imperialist one, aiming to penetrate, subdue, and reorient wholly different people, cultures, and nations within a value framework created in the United States.

We do not need the Pentagon Papers of the Nixon Administration. We already have them. We can already guess the plans for more years of US intervention by looking carefully at news dispatches, at public statements, and at a series of semiofficial and semisecret documents which are already available.

The Nixon–Kissinger Fraud: Vietnamization Is Nothing New

Nixon and his policy architect Henry Kissinger have changed America's methods in Indochina but not the goals: a pro-Western client state in South Vietnam, US access to military bases and trade opportunities in Southeast Asia. They are as deceitful and barbaric a pair as Lyndon Johnson and W. W. Rostow and deserve the same political fate: defeat, isolation, and retirement. But lest we place too much importance on individual qualities or stylistic differences between different officials, it is important to see certain continuities between the Johnson and Nixon administrations.

Because of the "Vietnamization" rhetoric and US troop withdrawals, it is widely accepted that Nixon is carrying out a "new" policy. But with the help of the Pentagon Papers, we can see that the Nixon–Kissinger policy was demanded in 1968 by the troubled situation in which the US government was trapped. Nixon and Kissinger, seen from this perspective, inherited roles which were nearly predetermined.

First, Vietnamization was an economic imperative. The 1965 prophecy of Lyndon Johnson that "both guns and butter" could be afforded was a proven impossibility by the spring of 1968. Maintaining a single frontline American soldier in Vietnam was costing $90,000; direct war costs were running $30 billion annually from 1965–1968. Political concern about the war's cost did not begin with Nixon. It was basic right from the beginning of the 1965 escalation. Johnson, like Nixon four years later, doubted that the American public would pay for the war through higher taxes. With that option closed, Johnson chose a short-run alternative of borrowing. The US budget deficit, approximately $0 in 1965, rose to $25 billion in 1968. The defense spending for Vietnam, within a

1965 economy which operated at relatively high employment and capacity, caused an immediate inflation. Consumer costs rose at a 7 percent rate after 1965. The transfer of workers from consumer goods to defense production not only aggravated inflation, but weakened the US international trade position: after 1965, because of overseas military spending and increased reliance on imports, the American balance of payments ratio became negative. The Senate Foreign Relations Committee on June 30, 1971, described the 1966 inflation as the worst experienced since that immediately following the end of World War II. Additional problems they said were "spiralling interest rates, severe money shortages, a collapse in the housing industry, a general slowdown in overall economic activity after nine years of rapid and sustained economic expansion, and severe distortions in the nation's financial markets." Only the expectation of a quick Vietnam victory made it possible to take these economic risks in 1965. When the prospect of that victory clearly collapsed in the Tet Offensive of 1968, the only option remaining was that of a "cheaper" long term war. Thus the economic reasons for Vietnamization were determined before Nixon entered office.

Second, the 1965–68 military strategy of the US had clearly failed by the beginning of Nixon's term. An American defeat during the Tet Offensive was a *"very near thing,"* according to a memo in the Pentagon Papers from Earl Wheeler, chairman of the Joint Chiefs of Staff. As it was, Alain C. Enthoven, the director of the Pentagon's Office of Systems Analysis, wrote privately that the Tet Offensive "appears to have *killed the [pacification] program for once and for all."* He summarized the miserable failure of the US this way:

> . . . despite a massive influx of 500,000 US troops, 1.2 million tons of bombs a year, 400,000 attack sorties per year, 200,000 enemy KIA [killed in action] in three years, 20,000 US KIA, etc., our control of the countryside and the

defense of the urban areas is now essentially at pre-August, 1965, levels. We have achieved stalemate at a high commitment. *A new strategy must be sought.*

The high-level group chosen in early 1968 to seek that "new strategy" was headed by Defense Secretary Clark Clifford, an intimate business and political adviser to Presidents since the beginning of the Cold War. The Clifford group stressed the folly of the US continuing to substitute its power for a dubious South Vietnamese government and recommended that US influence should be used "to buy the time" during which the Saigon regime "can develop effective capability," a clear foreshadowing of military Vietnamization.

The policy changes proposed to Lyndon Johnson as early as 1966 by Robert McNamara are similar to those Nixon would carry out in 1969. McNamara, now considered something of a "dove" because of his disenchantment with the bombing, is revealed in the very Pentagon Papers he commissioned to be obsessed more by considerations of cost and rational self-interest than by moral feelings. In an October 14, 1966, report to Johnson, the first in which he expressed doubts, he concludes with words that Kissinger could have penned:

> . . . the solution lies in girding, openly, for a longer war and in taking actions immediately which will in 12 to 18 months give clear evidence that the continuing costs and risks to the American people are *acceptably limited, that the formula for success has been found, and that the end of the war is merely a matter of time.*

McNamara's stress was not on getting out, but on changing the priority from the air war on the North to the ground war in the South, particularly through "pacification" and the build-up of the GVN forces.

An even more complete "Vietnamization" position was

taken consistently from the beginning of the US escalation by Undersecretary of State George Ball, the Administration "dove" who advocated "cutting our losses" in a July 1, 1965, memo. Ball favored restricting American troops to "advising and assisting the South Vietnamese"; holding American troop levels at 72,000 (nearly what Nixon plans for summer, 1972); maintaining US forces in defensive positions; continued limited bombing of the North; secret talks leading to negotiations, offering the "Viet Cong *some* hope of achieving *some* of their political objectives through *local* elections or some other device"; ending the war through a cease-fire which would leave the Saigon army intact; reassuring America's other Asian allies through greater economic and military assistance.

Not only did Clifford, McNamara, McNaughton, and Ball anticipate Nixon's strategy, but so also did the authors of the Pentagon Papers themselves. Widely thought to be "doves," the Pentagon intellectuals actually conclude their several-thousand-page history (the edition released by Senator Gravel) with an assessment, delivered in 1968, which seems like a script for the coming four years of the Nixon Administration:

> [the] road to peace would be at least as dependent upon South Vietnamese political development as it would be on American arms . . . American forces would remain in South Vietnam to prevent defeat of the government by communist forces and to provide a shield behind which that government could rally, become effective, and win the support of its people.

Besides the battlefield shambles, and a deterioration of GI morale, American planners were equally concerned with the corrosive effects the war was having on American society —another future Nixon concern. The Clifford group expressed worry at "growing disaffection," "increased defiance of the draft," "growing unrest in the cities" of America. But the most vivid statement of this fear of domestic repercussion came from McNamara's assistant, John McNaughton, who wrote to his boss:

> A feeling is widely and strongly held that *"the Establishment" is out of its mind*. The feeling is that we are trying to impose some US image on distant peoples we cannot understand (anymore than we can the younger generation here at home). Related to this feeling is the *increased polarization* that is taking place in the US with *seeds of the worst split in our people in more than a century*.

But if the stage was set for Nixon and Kissinger to carry out necessary changes in Vietnam policy, they were well chosen by history for their parts. Based on their past careers, there is no reason to think either would "abandon" the US commitment in Indochina. For years, both have advocated a hard-line policy in Vietnam. Through the changing forms of America's Vietnam involvement, both men have maintained a constant advocacy of a strong commitment. The necessity for drastic changes in method would appeal to them, as both fancy themselves experts in power politics and deception, and both model themselves after earlier creators of "eras of stable peace" based on new international alliances, Nixon after Woodrow Wilson, Kissinger after Metternich.

Nixon's earliest views on Vietnam could be embarrassing in the light of his present policy, since in 1954 as Vice President he opposed a French plan for "Vietnamizing" the war. *Life* magazine reported on August 3, 1954, that US officials were

> in deep discussion of a series of proposals by General Henri Navarre, commander-in-chief in Indochina, that the war be increasingly turned over to the Vietnamese themselves, permitting France to reduce the burden on its manpower and economy.

Nixon opposed this "Vietnamization" doctrine, declaring to the French in Hanoi in November, 1953, that "it is impossible to lay down arms until victory is completely won." On April 16, 1954, he claimed "the Vietnamese lack the ability to conduct a war by themselves or govern themselves," and said American ground troops should be sent if necessary. Nixon continued pushing a hard line in the sixties, and educated himself about Vietnam by traveling there at least five times, apparently as an attorney for Pepsi Cola at times as well as writing for *Reader's Digest*.

He belittled President Kennedy's 1962 build-up of US forces in Saigon as perhaps "too little too late," and in April, 1964, advocated attacking communist bases in North Vietnam and Laos. In January, 1965, he favored bombing and shelling the Ho Chi Minh Trail and staging areas in North Vietnam and Laos. In September, 1965, he proposed increased ground and air operations, including "military targets in the Hanoi area"; at the same time, *The New York Times* reported: "Mr. Nixon said he regarded the decision whether to retaliate directly on Communist China as contingent on the depth of the provocation." In August, 1966, Nixon advocated a 25 percent increase in US ground forces and hinted that the irrigation system of North Vietnam perhaps should be bombed. Right up to the devastating year of reconsideration—1968—Nixon was advocating slightly more "militarist" solutions than Johnson.

These Vietnam views were backed by occasional statements by Nixon of his philosophy that America should be a "Pacific power." In a 1967 *Foreign Affairs* article, "Asia After Vietnam," Nixon's declaration that *"our ideals and our interests propel us westward across the Pacific"* echoed and seemed to fulfill the 1903 forecast of Theodore Roosevelt that "the empire that shifted from the Mediterranean will, in the lifetime of those now children, bid fair to shift once more

[13]

westward to the Pacific." Speaking to a New York business-men's group in 1965, Nixon cited China as the main enemy who might turn the Pacific instead into a "Red Sea": ". . . the confrontation in Vietnam is, in the final analysis, between the United States and Communist China." If China should "gain from their aggression [in Asia] they will be encouraged to try it again . . . those who advocate the hard line in Peking . . . will have won the day . . . and we shall be confronted with other Vietnams in Asia." In 1967, already preparing for the moment of reopening ties with Peking, Nixon wrote:

> Dealing with Red China is something like trying to cope with the more explosive ghetto elements in our own country. In each case a potentially destructive force has to be curbed; in each case an outlaw element has to be brought within the law; in each case dialogues have to be opened; in each case aggression has to be restrained while education proceeds; and, not least, in neither case can we afford to let those now self-exiled from society stay exiled forever.

At the same time, Nixon told his *Foreign Affairs* readers exactly whose Asian interests the US should be supporting—those countries which have "discovered and applied the les-sons of America's own economic success," that is, a *"prime reliance on private enterprise"* and *"receptivity to foreign in-vestment."* Chief among these lands would be Japan, which Nixon in 1965 called "the biggest prize of all," the only Asian state with the "possible chance to counterbalance China." Long before becoming President, Nixon openly favored the remilitarizing of Japan for its role in the Pacific strategy.

It was not until the year of the Tet Offensive and the presidential election that Nixon started altering his rhetoric on Vietnam to suit the new reality. His selection of Henry Kissinger as foreign policy adviser was a major sign to many that he was adopting a different strategy. Kissinger, after all, had a history of apparent differences with Nixon. Kissinger became famous in the fifties for advocating the use of nuclear weapons in "limited" wars, differing with the "massive retaliation" concept of John Foster Dulles, whom Nixon admired. Kissinger was long the foreign policy adviser for the Rockefeller interests, and authored the Rockefeller "peace in Vietnam" plank in the 1968 Republican primaries. When Nixon chose Rockefeller's aide to be his national security assistant, therefore, it seemed to many doves to be a sign of moderation of Nixon's views. In retrospect, the "new Nixon" is only a man who has abandoned his smalltown entrepreneurial past (except for public relations) and identified himself completely with the world of multi-national corporations and eastern capital which Rockefeller represents. This is most apparent in Nixon's change in the last decade from a China Lobby extremist to an instrument of the more sophisticated overtures to the Chinese which the Rockefeller interests have long proposed. Nixon confesses his "change" with surprising frankness in an interview reprinted in the July 27, 1970, Department of State *Bulletin*:

> I know that what is called cold-war rhetoric isn't fashionable these days and I am not engaging in it, because I am quite practical.

A close look at Kissinger's public statements should discourage anyone from believing that either "Vietnamization" or the new US China policy means a real departure from stern American anti-communism and willingness to go to war.

In the fifties, Kissinger took hard-line positions on both Korea and Vietnam. In the first case, Kissinger believed the US should have "pushed back the Chinese armies even to the narrow neck of the Korean peninsula" so as to administer "a setback to communist power in its first trial at arms with the free world." This would have "caused China to question the value of its Soviet alliance, while the USSR would have been confronted with the dilemma of whether it was 'worth' an all-out war to prevent a limited defeat of its ally." Is this not the same pattern Kissinger is pursuing in 1972, with North Vietnam being made to "question" its relationship to Peking, and the Chinese made to choose between tolerating a limited defeat in Vietnam and "all-out war"?

In Vietnam, as in Korea, Kissinger believed the US was confronted with a nibbling form of communist expansion. Reliance on a "massive retaliation" capability (total war with the Soviet Union) was too great a risk, given the objectives, and the US lacked a "graduated" military capability. "We saw no military solution to the Indochinese crisis without accepting risks which we were reluctant to confront," he wrote in *Nuclear Weapons and Foreign Policy*. The dilemma was expressed in the nineteenth century by Bismarck, the imperialist statesman about whom Kissinger wrote his thesis, as follows:

> We live in a wondrous time in which the strong is weak because of his moral scruples and the weak grows strong because of his audacity.

"A strategy of limited war might reverse or at least arrest this trend," Kissinger wrote of Korea and Indochina. "Limited war is thus not an alternative to massive retaliation, but its complement."

The essentials of what became "Vietnamization" were contained a decade before in Kissinger's writings. As a "balance of power" theorist he envisioned a system of US-sponsored regional alliances. He had preferred a complete "Pax Americana" early in the Cold War when, he wrote, the US "underestimated the bargaining power inherent in our industrial potential and our nuclear superiority" over the Soviets. But by the sixties, he recognized the inevitability of a "multipolar" world, and the need for a flexible US diplomatic–

military strategy. This would involve "local defense" capabilities among America's allies, in a free-world network dominated by the US, because the US "alone" is "strong enough physically and psychologically to play a global role." For the seventies he forecast that America's role "will be to contribute to a structure that will foster the initiative of others." The US contribution should not be the "sole or principal effort, but it should make the difference between success or failure." This is exactly the Guam Doctrine as announced by Nixon.

Behind this Western alliance, and behind any "era of negotiations" Nixon and Kissinger might envision, is the fundamental factor of military force, the ultimate determinant of world power. Both men are ardent subscribers to this theory, though Nixon explains it more religiously than Kissinger, as seen in this personal interview with *The New York Times* on November 3, 1970:

> I can assure you *my words are those of a devoted pacifist.* . . . *If I lived in another country that wanted to be sure and retain its right to self-determination, I would say "Thank God the United States exists at this moment in history."* We are not bent on conquest, nor on threatening others. But *we do have a nuclear umbrella that can protect others.* We could be a terrible threat to the world if we were to lose that restraint.

Even this disclaimer of power contains its contradiction, for how can a nation have "self-determination" if it is dependent on American nuclear power and "restraint" for its freedom. That is the freedom of 1984 with Big Brother as protector.

Kissinger speaks more with the tongue of the political scientist, but the conclusion is the same. Not only has he advocated using the nuclear threat in relations with other nuclear powers, but against nonnuclear ones with vast resources of manpower if necessary:

> The problem of limited nuclear war arises primarily in actions against nuclear powers or *against powers with vast resources of manpower which are difficult to overcome with conventional technology.*

Kissinger's threatening attitude was brought to bear on the Vietnam question in a *Foreign Affairs* article published in January, 1969, the first month of the Nixon Administration. He decried the lack of a "political corollary" to America's military strength; that is, the lack of a viable government in South Vietnam. Hanoi was far more able than the US, he acknowledged, "to design military strategies for political ends." America has been "unable so far to create a political structure that could survive military opposition from Hanoi after we withdraw."

But while room for political bargaining *inside* Vietnam was unfavorable to the US, Kissinger believed that the US held a superior hand against its Vietnamese enemies within the *military* power framework. "We are so powerful that Hanoi is simply unable to defeat us militarily," and "since it cannot force our withdrawal, it must negotiate about it."

This is the stance of a bully disguised by Ivy League double-talk. In his strategic writing on the use of threats, Kissinger once wrote that where America cannot get its way, it can *"pose risks for the enemy out of proportion to the objectives under dispute."* This cute statement presumably means that the "objectives under dispute" for the other side—national independence, for instance—will be compromised if the "risk" posed is, say, genocide. Or instead of genocide, perhaps a more limited torture, the formula for which is to apply "graduated amounts of destruction" alternately with "breathing spaces for political contacts." Applied to Vietnam, this doctrine means military pressure, including "risks out of proportion to the objectives" of the other side, should be relentlessly continued, with periodic inquiries or negotiations ("breathing spaces") in case the Vietnamese have had enough.

Why does this war mean so much? Kissinger answers in much the same power terms that his humiliated predecessors in the Johnson Administration did: it is a matter of *the American image of power, the American will.* The commitment of 500,000 troops in itself *"settles the issue of the importance of Vietnam."* What is at stake is *"confidence in American promises"* for "other nations can gear their actions to ours only if they can count on our *steadiness."* Why a continuation of a wasteful and losing war will inspire "confidence" in America, why any other clients would be impressed with the "steadiness" of US destruction, is unanswered. Kissinger's arrogance is a taken-for-granted position, one exactly in keeping with that of an earlier Pentagon adviser, John McNaughton, seven years before. The Pentagon Papers reveal that the American aim, in McNaughton's view, should be 70 percent to "avoid a humiliating US defeat (to our reputation as 'guarantor')," only 20 percent to stop Chinese expansion, and only 10 percent "to permit the people of South Vietnam to enjoy a better, freer way of life." Elaborating one year later, McNaughton added:

> The reasons why we *went* into Vietnam to the present depth are varied; but they are now largely academic. Why we have not withdrawn from Vietnam is, by all odds, one reason: . . . *to preserve our reputation as a guarantor, and thus to preserve our effectiveness in the rest of the world.*

If this position is maintained—as it has been through the whole Nixon period—for the indefinite future, it is difficult to imagine how the US would ever withdraw its financial and military stake from Southeast Asia, for, as we shall see, America's client states there are so critically weak that the guerrilla forces would come to power, in the wake of US withdrawal, thus damaging the US role of guarantor. The only "peace terms" which would leave the "guarantor" role intact would be terms of surrender for the other side, terms assuring continued status to the corrupt and tyrannical US-sponsored regimes in Saigon, Phnom Penh, Vientiane, and Bangkok, terms perpetuating the Pacific power of an American empire.

On the Battlefield:
No Winding Down for Asians

The Indochina war is "winding down" only for American GIs. After a decade (1961–71) in which American deaths were 45,000 and total casualties 400,000—more casualties than World War I, twice that of Korea, one third that of World War II—the toll has declined under Nixon's policy. Here are the approximate figures given by the Department of Defense:

	US dead	US wounded
1969	9,000	70,000
1970	4,000	30,000
1971	1,400	10,000
Total	14,400	110,000

There is little reason to be relieved by these figures. A total of almost 15,000 Americans have been killed and 110,-000 wounded during the "winding down" of the war. Dying is the same during escalation or de-escalation. Few parents would accept the explanation from Kissinger that their son's death was necessary to impress other nations with America's "steadiness" in keeping promises.

Nor do these figures mean that the US will not suffer further casualties of a significant number in South Vietnam. The shrinking numbers of American troops in South Vietnam are at the mercy of the liberation forces in the South if and when the withdrawal of American troops fails to continue. Neil Sheehan suggested in the January 16, 1972, *The New York Times* that "the sharp drop in American casualties in Vietnam has been achieved to a large extent with the tacit consent of the enemy," and recalled that "in one attack on an American artillery base in the central region last March . . . the enemy killed 33 American soldiers and wounded 76 in one hour."

Nor does the fact that American casualties are going down mean that the United States is going to withdraw *all* its troops. Senator Thomas Eagleton reported on March 12, 1971, that US generals in Vietnam informed him that "the plans under which they were operating called for a *residual American force* indefinitely into the future and for a protracted period of massive American air power." There never has been an official revision of that position.

Above all, the ground war is not ending, not winding down, for the people of Asia, for the Vietnamese in particular. US figures show 470,000 ARVN and 715,000 enemy *killed* in the last decade: a total of *1.2 million* Vietnamese military personnel on all sides. Under Nixon, the ground war has expanded to Cambodia and escalated in Laos. The casualty figures today remain *constant* as fierce fighting continues all over Asia. By US count:

DEATH TOLL IN SOUTH VIETNAM, 1969–71

	ARVN (Saigon)	Enemy
1969	21,000	157,000
1970	23,000	103,000
1971	21,000	97,000
Total	65,000	357,000

These totals under Nixon are about twice the numbers of Vietnamese killed on either side during any year of the John-

son Administration except the last; only the climactic year 1968 resulted in more Vietnamese dead, 27,000 ARVN and 180,000 "enemy." The total ARVN casualties, counting both dead and wounded, in Nixon's first three years has been approximately 250,000; the figure under Johnson, from 1966 through 1968, was far less, 170,000 (and was even less—a total of 130,000—during the first *four* years of Johnson, 1964 through 1967). The ARVN "body count" under Nixon, running between 200 and 300 deaths per week, is *far more than the US government found politically acceptable when the corpses were white.*

The "enemy" death tolls do not include those killed in Cambodia, Laos, North Vietnam, and Thailand. The apparent decline in "enemy" killed under Nixon, from 157,000 in 1969 to 97,000 for 1971, is misleading as well. It reflects the expansion of the ground war beyond South Vietnam (therefore beyond which enemy bodies are counted), and also the existence of peaceful accommodation between NLF and weaker ARVN troops in certain parts of South Vietnam. This is admitted in a 1970 RAND/Pentagon study by Stephen Hosmer:

> . . . much of the accommodation which exists at these levels is asymmetrical, in that it benefits the local units or organization of the Viet Cong more than it does the GVN's. . . .
> In many such contested areas, the Viet Cong consider the GVN's presence to be effectively "neutralized" and are reluctant to upset the existing situation lest . . . they draw unwarranted attention . . .

It would be wrong to assume that the slight "lull" in the ground war in South Vietnam represents anything more than these accommodations plus smaller, less-publicized, guerrilla operations by the NLF. According to North Vietnamese statistics, from the beginning of Nixon's tenure until June, 1971, there were 50,000 "mopping-up" operations of battalion size and larger, and more than 3,000 hamlets were "blotted out" or "heavily devastated," *one fourth* the total number of hamlets in South Vietnam, and "hundreds of Son My-type massacres" were perpetrated. Millions of peasants were forced to move to US-controlled areas from their homes in the five northernmost provinces of South Vietnam in the same period. Under Nixon, according to *Time,* the US has supplied the South Vietnamese government with 640,000 M-16s, 20,000 machine guns, 34,-000 grenade launchers, 10,000 81-mm. mortars, 200 tanks, 1,000 armored vehicles, 44,000 jeeps, 1600 naval vessels, and 850 bombers (1,200 expected by 1972).

Daniel Ellsberg points out that *all* of these deaths on *all* sides are an American responsibility. If the Saigon client state would not have fought without US assistance since 1954, as he says, then the US is responsible for killing both those it opposes and those it sponsors.

This American responsibility for the deaths of Asians will continue. The Saigon regime already has one million men under arms, with American military aid projected for the next ten years at as much as $9 billion. In Cambodia, which the President describes as "the Nixon Doctrine in pure form," the pitiful Lon Nol army has grown from 30,000 in 1970 to 180,000 in 1971 (including ten-year-olds), and American officials envision 306,000 regular and 550,000 paramilitary troops by 1977, a total of 856,000 troops which would be *50 percent of all that country's adult males! (Washington Post,* October 14, 1971).

In Laos, there are 30,000 Thai mercenaries and tens of thousands of Meo tribesmen on the US payroll, in addition to a Royal Lao army of 50,000 (also funded and supported by the US). The South Vietnamese NLF reported in 1971 that the American-sponsored force in Laos had already doubled, and the RLG troop level was going to be increased to 70,000. The Meo forces in Laos cannot be increased, for, according

to many reports, their total numbers have been so badly decimated that their further existence as a people will be threatened if they continue as mercenaries for the CIA.

The bizarre effect of this Nixon policy of funding mercenaries, in this case Asians to fight Asians, is that it begins to
return the United States to a policy close to that of its "mother
country," the British Empire, at its height of power. The American Declaration of Independence specifically rebukes King
George III for "transporting large armies of foreign mercenaries to complete the works of death, desolation and tyranny,
already begun with circumstances of cruelty and perfidy
scarcely paralleled in the most barbarous ages."

The ugly heart of the Nixon ground-war strategy has been
an increased "pacification" program. This has long lost even
its euphemistic purpose of "winning hearts and minds" through
missionary good works. It has become a police-state operation,
consisting mainly of countrywide round-ups, concentration
camps, police build-ups, expanding prisons, and new technology for population control. Early in his administration,
Nixon called for advice from Sir Robert Thompson, the British
agent with successful credentials from Malaysia. Thompson
took two secret trips to South Vietnam in 1969–70 to super-
vise the new police build-up. On April 4, 1971, *The New
York Times* reported the "most ambitious and costly pacification program yet planned for Vietnam." The US contribution
for 1971 alone was $1 billion. The US Civil Operations and
Rural Development Support (CORDS) agency allocation to
the South Vietnamese police jumped by over 25 percent, from
$21 million in 1970 to $27.3 million in 1971. The South Vietnamese police, who numbered 16,000 in 1960, reached 97,000
in 1971, and 120,000 in 1972 as US troop withdrawals pro-
ceeded.

One diabolic part of "pacification," increased under
Nixon, is called "Operation Phoenix." It aims at the killing of

NLF political personnel in the cities and villages. It requires what the US calls the "most foolproof classification scheme yet developed," a system of identification cards and checkpoints that makes South Vietnam more like a minimum security prison than a civilian society. Under the South Vietnamese constitution, the police can act against anyone considered a "threat to national security." There are as many as 400,000 persons in jail under these kinds of laws; half of them have never been tried before a court. John de Pemberton of the American Civil Liberties Union says the treatment in these prisons includes "the most brutal of the methods of torture known to history." Over $6 million in aid goes for US prison advisers and prison maintenance; under Nixon, $100 million is being spent on prison enlargement.

The Phoenix program last year took credit for "neutralizing" 88,000 and killing 22,000 "Viet Cong cadre," but is widely considered to be more effective against President Thieu's political opponents than against the NLF, who have been evading similar repressions for years. The *Washington Post,* on December 14, 1971, reported the complete failure of the Phoenix program.

Nevertheless, *The New York Times* reports, the US continues to press the Phoenix-type plans: the "national police must play a vital role in the program designed to track down and kill or capture Viet Cong *political* officials." This is surely one reason the NLF cannot accept Nixon's offer of "free elections" in the South; they would necessarily expose themselves to the CIA-trained Phoenix killers!

Year after year American hopes about pacification (like French hopes before them) rise briefly, then fall. The failure of this program means the failure of Kissinger's hope for an eventual "political corollary" to US military power. Yet fail it has. In the same article revealing the escalated pacification program, *The New York Times* quoted a US report acknowledging that the "military region that includes 15 provinces south of Saigon and in the Mekong Delta poses the most serious security problem." This is the most populous section of South Vietnam, and an area from which US ground forces mainly withdrew in 1969. An equally ominous problem for the US is that, after years of attempted pacification, not only have they failed in the countryside but the South Vietnamese government itself, by a CIA estimate, has become congested with *30,000 NLF agents!*

A final point on pacification, the fraud of Vietnamization, is further underscored by the fact that this pacification program is top-heavy with difficult to replace American technicians. CORDS, for instance, is staffed by 8,000 highly trained personnel from the CIA and the US Department of Defense.

The failure of pacification reflects the general failure of the ground war. Enough has been exposed of the ground war in South Vietnam to convince any objective observer that the NLF commands the initiative and always has. The fact that US troops were introduced in the first place to stave off an ARVN defeat (confirmed by the Pentagon Papers) does not bode well for the poor ARVN as these US troops withdraw without having defeated the NLF.

But not enough people realize the same process of successful guerrilla war is taking place in Laos and Cambodia. After the US–ARVN invasion of Laos in February, 1971, for example, a staff report to the Senate Foreign Relations Committee concluded:

> Most observers in Laos say that from the military point of view the situation there is growing steadily worse and the *initiative seems clearly to be in the hands of the enemy.*
>
> Since Lam Son 719 [the invasion code name] *more Lao territory has come under enemy control,* and there are about three regiments more of North Vietnamese forces in southern Laos than there were before the Lam Son operation.

> . . . *the Pathet Lao and North Vietnamese are in the strongest military position they have ever enjoyed* . . .
>
> . . . the area under government control shrinks steadily, the cost to the United States rises, the Pathet Lao consolidate their hold on territories no longer under government control and the Lao government's professed policy of neutralism continues to hang by the single human thread of Prime Minister Souvanna Phouma. He in turn seems to be increasingly isolated from other powerful political figures in his country who wish to involve the United States, or the Thai, even further in the defense of what remains of their country, knowing that *they cannot possibly defend it themselves.*

The Laos situation one year later is even worse for the United States. As part of a 1971–72 ground offensive, which *Aviation Week* said "may surpass the 1968 Tet drive," the Pathet Lao took the Plain of Jars in northern Laos in December, 1971. They destroyed seven Thai battalions (250 men per battalion), as well as Meo and Lao firebases nearby, then began the encirclement and siege of the CIA-sponsored secret base at Long Cheng. The US promptly flew its precious electronic equipment out of Long Cheng, which had been its *operations center* in northern Laos, and left the pitiful Meo and Lao troops to withstand the siege (with heavy US air support). At the same time, the Pathet Lao swept over the strategic Bolovens Plateau to the south. Still holding the Ho Chi Minh Trail, the Pathet Lao and North Vietnamese troops thus obtained nearly complete control of the countryside in Laos.

In Cambodia at the same time, the US-supported regime was crumbling also. From the beginning, Lon Nol's dictatorship (he dissolved the parliament finally in November, 1971) was disgracefully weak, and *Le Monde* had called it the "feeble link" in the US chain in Indochina. *The New York Times* reported on June 27, 1971, that "the Vietnamese Communists [read: Cambodian United Front] are still in control of three fourths of the sparsely populated countryside." *Le Monde* reported that the Khmer "Reds" seem able "to move about as they like. . . . In addition to numerous towns, the rural areas are largely free from the authority in Phnom Penh." Lon Nol with a minuscule army in the beginning and virtually no legitimacy after overthrowing the popular Sihanouk, was forced to rely on Saigon mercenary troops to defend Cambodia. They in turn acted out their traditional anti-Cambodia prejudices; on the infamous night of January 31, 1971, for instance, they placed roadblocks in Phnom Penh and began robbing Cambodians of money and jewelry, and their pillaging was even more devastating in the countryside.

The Cambodians under Lon Nol set out on a fatal attempt in August, 1971, to retake the countryside north of Phnom Penh, in an operation named "Chenla II." By December, according to *The New York Times,* half their 20,000 troops were "virtually destroyed as a fighting unit" (12/3/71). They had lost their headquarters at Baray, and in one battle, November 13, admitted to 1,100 casualties. When 50,000 ARVN troops invaded Cambodia to the south, supposedly to relieve the pressure on "Chenla II," they found no enemies to fight. But they did panic at reports that the NLF, now behind their back in South Vietnam, were beginning attacks on Saigon which was only guarded by "inept" ARVN troops (*Christian Science Monitor,* November 23, 1971). Therefore the ARVN abandoned their Cambodian relief mission to return hastily to the Saigon area. When the ARVN left their base at Krek, 2,400 Cambodian troops panicked at being left behind—in their own country!—and fled with them into South Vietnam. "North Vietnamese" troops were reported to have established a new base in the Krek area shortly after.

This is the pattern of military shambles all across Indochina as of the spring of 1972. The US is withdrawing troops and leaving a vacuum. The ARVN, whose ability to pacify their own country has been tried unsuccessfully once before (1956–64), are supposed to guard not only South Vietnam but are also to be a mercenary spearhead to aid the pathetic Cambodian and Royal Laotian armies. The ARVN thus become imperialist invaders into two countries while being spread thin across their own (desertion and draft evasion are at "epidemic proportions," *Time* reported on February 7, 1972). In their one major test of fire outside South Vietnam, during the February, 1971, Lam Son "incursion" into Laos, they were smashed and, running on foot and hanging from helicopter landing rods, driven back into South Vietnam. At the same time, in a less publicized invasion of Cambodia, their commander was killed in a helicopter crash and their ground operations went in circles. If they attempt to return to Cambodia or Laos today, the same fate probably awaits them, while, in their rear, the NLF can move more easily around Saigon, the Central Highlands, and the coastal areas of South Vietnam. But if the ARVN remain to defend South Vietnam, they will soon see the triumph of liberation armies in Laos and Cambodia. This is the classic dilemma of guerrilla war for the armies of repression which lack wide popular support: to concentrate their forces allows the other side to expand the scope of attack, while to disperse their forces in frantic pursuit results in a dangerous overextension. This is what happened to the French at Dien Bien Phu, the US at Tet in 1968, and what has become the crisis of the whole Indochinese battleground as the seventies begin.

So the fraud of "Vietnamization" is the claim that America's tattered mercenaries can stand alone. One by one, they will meet the terrible fate of the Meo highlanders in Laos who have been used by the CIA to fight their traditional lowland enemies and who have suffered near-extinction in the process. The Royal Lao and Cambodian armies are too weak to exist without Thai and South Vietnamese support, respectively, and they rely more on US air power than on their own ground operations for survival. The ARVN, touted as the centerpiece of the new Nixon strategy, are one of the largest armies in the world, but lack any other impressive qualities. Even the latest *Time* analysis of insiders' opinions (February 7, 1972) gives the ARVN's 600,000 regular forces only a "fair shot" against their enemies, and then only "if they have ample air support." "But no one knows what to expect from the untried irregulars" who number 500,000 and supposedly guard the "vital outposts" of the countryside. As for the 500,000-man militia, the Popular Self-Defense Force, "they are assumed to be so infiltrated by the VC that many . . . outposts will not allow PSDF troops in after dark."

In fact these mercenaries are so undependable that it cannot be imagined that the US really is depending on their prowess to stave off "communist expansion." They go on few, if any, offensive operations; when they do, it is usually only to draw out the enemy so the Air Force can attack. Otherwise, their duties seem to be the removal of unarmed villagers, and the guarding of towns, outposts, and bases: hardly the functions of a successful army!

Three possible explanations of US intentions exist: (1) US planners know their mercenaries are inept, and merely want to withdraw American forces before the other side sweeps into power. But the American stake in Asia is too great to make that plausible. (2) US planners are deluded into believing their own rhetoric and therefore will be stunned when their mercenaries collapse in a year or two. The Pentagon Papers show that American intelligence is quite accurate about the state of battlefield forces, though its advice is not always followed. If US planners are deluded now, however, then a major escalation is probable when the illusion is broken by the Indochinese liberation armies. (3) US planners know the quality of their mercenaries quite well, and therefore depend on American air power and the threat of escalation, rather than Vietnamization, to stave off defeat in Indochina. This last alternative best describes the reality of what is happening today.

The Air War: Substituting Technology for American Troops

The air war is the primary form of direct American intervention in Indochina. US officials have said the air war will continue indefinitely, and be essentially unlimited, not only to protect American troops remaining in South Vietnam but also to protect the client regimes in Saigon, Phnom Penh, and Vientiane.

For the past two years, there has been a relative silence in the press about this bombing campaign. Then with the resumption of heavy attacks on North Vietnam during Christmas, 1971, public attention focused again on the nature of the air attacks. An absurd and depressing debate arose about how much the Nixon Administration was bombing Indochina. A study originating at Cornell University suggested that the level of bombing had not declined or wound down under Nixon. The Administration, clearly worried about public reaction to the strikes, quickly denounced the Cornell study, Secretary Laird claiming that "contrary to the impression that some have, we have substantially reduced the air activities in Southeast Asia." *The Wall Street Journal,* on January 15, supported Laird with the irrational insistence that the bombings "have helped cool the war rather than heat it" (could this have been the reason for the press silence on this issue for so long?). Expressing a contentedness which was missing during the Johnson bombing campaign, *The Wall Street Journal* advised its influential readership that "the Administration's success in winding down the ground war without debacle ought to earn it . . . a benefit of the doubt with respect to the air war as well."

It is difficult to imagine the scale of the air war because it is unprecedented in human history, the most concentrated bombing of civilian targets ever attempted. Not only is the air war distant and remote, and much of it secret, but we have neither the experience nor the language to grasp it. When the community of Guernica in Spain was bombed by the fascists thirty-five years ago, with eighty civilians killed in one raid, there was world outrage. Compare that fact to these:

A total of 11.5 million tons of air, ground, and sea munitions were detonated in Southeast Asia through 1970 (figures from the Senate Foreign Relations Committee). This was far more, even in 1970, than was dropped by the US during World War II. By 1972 the figure must be in the range of 14 million tons.

Of that total in 1970, six million tons were made up of air munitions alone: bombs, rockets, shells from aerial cannons.

In Korea, the US dropped one million tons of bombs; in World War II, two million tons on Europe and the Pacific theaters together.

Just since 1969, since the beginning of the Nixon Administration, the US has dropped three million tons on Indochina: six million pounds per day; 4,000 pounds per minute. All this dropped in about 1,000 sorties per day by a low-profile airborne force of 10,000 men at ten bases and on two or three aircraft carriers.

Under Nixon, more Indochinese people have been made targets of firepower and bombardment than at any time in the twenty-five-year history of American involvement.

The Nixon Administration from 1969 to 1971 dropped

more bombs on Indochina—3.1 million tons—than the Johnson Administration did in its last three years—2.8 million.

Under Nixon, only the bombing of South Vietnam has been diminished, a fact traceable to his widening of the scope of the war. In 1968, two thirds of America's bombs fell on South Vietnam; by 1971, two thirds were falling in Laos and Cambodia. Under Nixon the bombing of Laos has doubled, and the bombing of Cambodia—which was a few strikes per year under Johnson—has become constant. And recently under Nixon, the bombing of North Vietnam has escalated. The US officially admits about 215 bombings of the North, from the beginning of the Nixon Administration until February 1, 1972. But of this total, half were in 1971 (101), and at a rapidly increasing rate: 40 in November–December, 1971, and 32 in the first month of 1972. The North Vietnamese figures are much higher: 31,000 US reconaissance flights, at increasing rates; 2,700 tactical air strikes; 600 B52 strikes; a total of 185,000 demolition and blast bombs, 2,800 cluster bomb units and countless rockets since 1969 on their country.

There is no reason to believe the bombing campaign will slacken during "Vietnamization," although more of the planes will be flown by Vietnamese. The consequences of the bombing so far make the future seem unimaginably horrible.

High explosive bombs used by the United States range from 250 through *15,000 pounds* in weight. The 7.5 ton bomb will flatten an area the size of two football fields and create a 6,000-foot-high cloud.

Twenty million craters have been left on the landscape of Indochina, according to a study for the American Association for the Advancement of Science. Craters from B52 strikes are approximately forty-five feet wide and thirty feet deep; there are nearly three million of these craters today.

Defoliation through spraying with herbicides has also left fundamental damage. The cost of this "resource denial" program rose from $12.5 million in 1965–66 to $71 million at its height in 1968–69. Four million acres, one half the arable land of South Vietnam, were seriously affected, according to a 1967 report to the Japanese Science Council. Half the mangrove forests of the Mekong Delta have been permanently killed, and one fifth of the hardwood forests in South Vietnam damaged ("enough hardwood timber to supply the domestic construction market in South Vietnam for 30 years," according to E. W. Pfeiffer's report to the AAAS). In Laos, large areas have been made uninhabitable, and an estimated 179,000 acres of Cambodia have been affected since 1969. The ecological effects of this destruction already are beginning to appear: protective growth dies off, organic materials in the soil disappear, and the land turns bricklike in the sun.

The short- and long-term effects on human beings are frightening. Nearly 10 percent of South Vietnam's population has been sprayed *directly*. Johnson's chief science adviser once frankly admitted "it's all geared to move the people," but no official has confronted what happens to the people in the process. Millions of pounds of the chemical 2,4,5 T, a powerful tetrogen (which causes *fetus-deforming* effects), have been used in South Vietnam. This fact was revealed by the press in 1969, four years after it had been reported in a private National Institute of Health study. Experiments with mice show these chemicals to produce malformed fetuses and increases in cancer. When Saigon papers in 1969 began printing incredible pictures of malformed Vietnamese babies, under headlines such as "The Disease of Women Producing Stillborn Fetuses," and claiming this horror was causing "the noisiest discussion," the Thieu regime closed down the papers.

Even without these chemical agents, of course, the children of Vietnam would be threatened. A study in Biafra showed that after only two years of widespread adult malnutrition—a common malady in South Vietnam—*four of ten infants were born malformed.*

These are the grim meanings of the 1969 statement by an American officer that "we are fighting their birthrate" in Vietnam.

The Nixon Administration has tried to escape responsibility for the chemical warfare, and in December, 1970, ordered the phasing out of defoliation "step by step." The North Vietnamese War Crimes Commission insists that this chemical spraying has continued by means of a loophole permitting defoliation around US bases. What cannot be dropped from the air, in any case, can be used by ground forces, and the US has never ceased to use gas and toxic chemicals (and is training the ARVN in the same tactics). Nor has the process of destroying forests ended, but bulldozers have come to complement the chemical defoliants. Beginning in 1968, and increasing ever since, five American companies, with 150 bulldozers, have been destroying forests from dawn to dusk (the night is still too dangerous, which explains why the forests have to be leveled). *One thousand acres are leveled on an average day;* millions of acres have been destroyed to date.

Nixon has not changed the nature of the antipersonnel weapons used by the Air Force in Indochina; if anything, their use has been increased and constantly is being "perfected." Napalm and white phosphorus are still used in vast quantities. Their effect was described in the following blunt terms by a US pilot to the Welsh photographer Philip Jones Griffiths:

We sure are pleased with those backroom boys at Dow. The original product wasn't so hot—if the gooks were quick, they could scrape it off. So the boys started adding polystyrene—now it sticks like shit to a blanket. But then if the gooks jumped under water it stopped burning, so they started adding Willie Peter (WP-white phosphorus) so's to make it burn better. It'll even burn underwater now. And just one drop is enough, it'll keep burning right down to the bone so they die anyway from phosphorus poisoning.

The most widely used bombs are the antipersonnel fragmentation variety. These are devised for flesh, they cannot destroy steel or concrete. Their effect, since they severely wound more than kill, is to create a massive medical problem: hundreds of thousands of people with deep slice wounds from tiny pieces of metal often buried deep inside their bodies.

One of the fragmentation bombs, the Dragontooth, which can be dropped in quantities of 8,000 in one sortie, is described this way by Air Force personnel: "If a person steps on it, it could blow his foot off. If a truck runs over it, it won't blow the tire."

The most common ones, innocently nicknamed the "guava" and the "pineapple," release ball-bearing-sized pellets. Others release flechettes, sharp-edged pieces of metal. Another releases jagged fragments. The quantities are staggering. The "pineapple" and "guava," both small enough to hold in the hand, each contain 250 pellets which are released on explosion. One sortie alone will drop 1,000 "pineapples," which spew horizontally over an area the size of three football fields. The "guavas" are dropped by the hundreds from "mother bomb" containers; they explode in the air and travel diagonally toward the holes and bunkers where people are hiding; a single sortie will release 500,000 pellets.

It took several years to establish that fragmentation bombs were being used although we pay for the bombs and they are dropped in our name. The US government is supersensitive to publicity about its genocidal weapons, and clearly secretive about their nature. In fact, the government seems to be under no obligation to explain their experimental warfare techniques, much less present their weapons to the public for inspection. If it were not for the people of Asia upon whom these bombs are dropped, Americans probably would not be able to acquire and inspect them.

Since the technology of the air war is always developing, and since much of it is covered with secrecy, the public is never aware of the newest lethal systems being prepared or used. One which has been developed very extensively since 1969, about which we know very little, is the system of automated warfare known as the *electronic battlefield*. First conceived by Robert McNamara in 1966 as an "electronic wall" across the DMZ, the *electronic battlefield* finally came into full-scale use under Nixon.

This new electronic system contains supposed answers to Nixon's two major problems: how to stop a people's war —by destroying the people; and how to reduce American combat casualties—by automating the killers.

The principle of the electronic battlefield, called the "greatest invention since gunpowder" by Barry Goldwater, is quite simple. The landscape, in this case the Ho Chi Minh Trail and the liberated areas of Southeast Asia, is covered with small devices called sensors, developed by corporations like Sylvania and Honeywell. These detect vibrations, sounds, smells, and heat. They are all camouflaged to look like branches, plants, human feces. They transmit the supposed presence of enemy forces (or whoever or whatever triggers them) to giant computer centers in Thailand which flash the information to aircraft which are then electronically tracked to the target to release laser-guided or TV-guided bombs, called "smart bombs." In the vernacular of one Air Force commander:

> We wired up the Ho Chi Minh Trail like a pinball machine and we plug it in every night. Laos has been bugged with the most efficient system ever. Warfare has gone electronic.

[37]

General Westmoreland explained the strategic significance in 1969:

> On the battlefield of the future, enemy forces will be located, tracked and targeted almost instantaneously through the use of data links, computer-assisted intelligence evaluation, and automatic fire control. With first-round kill probabilities approaching certainty, and with surveillance devices that can continually track the enemy, *the need for large forces to fix the opposition physically will be less important.*

According to the Washington correspondent of the *Far Eastern Economic Review,* Michael Malloy, the electronic battlefield is mainly responsible for Nixon's success in Indochina. Malloy's January 29, 1972, article extolled the new system this way:

> Vietnamization is working. Its unsung hero is the transistor. Technology has temporarily won the day in Indochina. . . .
> This kind of war is infinitely preferable to Nixon because it is fought entirely from the air and utilizes the privileged sanctuaries of Thailand and the US Seventh Fleet. It costs few American casualties and is usually hidden from newsmen and other outsiders.

The electronic battlefield already is in operation, especially in southern Laos (the Ho Chi Minh Trail), the tricorner area where Laos, Cambodia, and South Vietnam join borders, and the DMZ. Although its main function is for the air war, it also has been widely used for ground security. Sensors are spread outside the perimeter of bases to detect guerrillas moving up for attacks. This supposedly permits an answer to the problems of Vietnam's feared night: sensors, infrared scopes, and other equipment turn the darkness into light, providing "eyes" to the US and GVN forces.

Already, however, this new system is the subject of controversy and conflicting claims. "One of the biggest problems is that it may be an indiscriminate weapon," Senator William

Proxmire complained on July 6, 1970. "The sensors cannot tell the difference between soldiers and women and children." In the November, 1970, hearings before a Senate subcommittee the Air Force's General Dean in effect agreed, then added an "assurance" that only a pure militarist could trust: "[our officers] use your best judgment. I think the commanders that I have known, if they had doubts, they wouldn't fire."

The importance of reducing American ground casualties is one of the key arguments used to support the electronic battlefield. Again and again the Senate hearings contain claims like these from top Air Force and Army officials:

> We are making unusual efforts to avoid having the American young man stand toe-to-toe, eyeball-to-eyeball, or even rifle-to-rifle against an enemy that may outnumber him on the battlefield.
>
> What is most important, gentlemen, is that we can gather this type of intelligence without exposing one American soldier to enemy action.

The Army's General Williamson claims the US will be able to "use one battalion where we had to use two before," and cites a "dramatically" improving ratio of GIs killed to enemy killed after 1968, due to the new sensors. It is also claimed that the 200 Americans killed in the Khe Sanh battle of early 1968 would have been doubled were it not for the sensors which were used, on a single day, to call several hundred air strikes, 500 artillery strikes, 80 radar-directed bombings, and 16 B52 missions.

The electronic battlefield even further depersonalizes a depersonalized war. This kind of war by machine makes the enemy less known to the American killer than ever before. Stationed on an aircraft carrier, the pilot never has to see the people he bombs. In the words of Eric Herter, son of the former Secretary of State and a Vietnam veteran who opposes the war, *"gooks become blips."*

Through the acoustic sensors these "blips" can be overheard talking. Like an electronic version of collecting hunting trophies, the Pentagon keeps a tape library in which one actually can hear unsuspecting Vietnamese and Pathet Lao talking on the Ho Chi Minh Trail, their voices intensifying as they discover a camouflaged sensor, and then their sounds wiped out in the crash of bombs on their position.

The Senate hearings provide another illuminating instance of how far the depersonalization process has gone, a case of killing not interfering even with breakfast. In February, 1969, during an operation near Dau Tieng, American support troops (cooks, clerks, mechanics) surprised and fought an NLF unit which had triggered the sensors one night and then, in General Williamson's glowing words:

> I have never seen a more confident group of cooks in my life who, after eliminating some seventy-eight of the enemy one night, served hot breakfast right on time the next morning.

Laos is the prime experimental battleground where the new technology is being tested. Americans there certainly must look like monsters from afar to the villagers. Since 1964 the US has been running a secret war through the CIA, AID, and other agencies, funding mercenary Thais as well as Royal Lao forces (at a cost of $400 million), and, most important, dropping two million tons of bombs (at a cost of $10 billion). This was never revealed to Congress, much less the public, until late 1969, and then only in sketchy detail. The Senate Foreign Relations Committee, for example, did not find out until May, 1971, that the US had been using B52s in northern Laos since February, 1970.

The US operates a parallel structure alongside its corrupt client state in Laos. The Laos government is "almost totally dependent on the US, perhaps more dependent on us than any government in the world," according to the same

Senate committee. Once underpopulated and therefore able to feed itself easily, Laos has become a rice importer (like all of America's Indochinese dependencies), and its trade balance is remarkable: $2 million in exports last year compared with $42 million worth of imported goods! The Lao government's budget for 1971 was $36.6 million; by contrast, the US spent nine times as much in Laos, $285 million, not including the cost of CIA operations, US bombing of northern and southern Laos, and the pay for Thai mercenaries. No wonder the US AID head is referred to as "the second prime minister of Laos."

With less than 1,000 personnel, according to most estimates, the US is running the kind of war which may be attempted elsewhere in the future: low visibility, low American casualties, reliance on mercenaries, plus a heavily funded bombing campaign.

Laos is the "most heavily bombed country in history" in the estimate of the *Washington Post*. It was frankly explained in *The New York Times*, October 1, 1969, that "the rebel economy and social fabric" is the main target. Robert Shaplen in *Foreign Affairs*, April, 1970, agreed that the bombing is "destroying the political and economic fabric of life in Pathet Lao areas"—equivalent in size to New York State, covering about two thirds of Laos, with 3,000–4,000 villages and one million people. A United Nations adviser, speaking of the entire country, has said the US planes are destroying "the material basis of civilian society." The Plain of Jars, for example, once contained 50,000 people and today is empty of everyone but soldiers. Although the Kennedy subcommittee on refugee problems has found that the dislocated villagers—numbering as many as 700,000 in a country of less than three million people—blame their dislocation on US bombing of their villages, the US government still routinely denies any bombing of civilian targets like villages.

Even though this technology appears invincible, the

truth is that it is not working very well in Indochina. The reason for its failure is that the problem of revolution is not technical but political. The sensors and surveillance systems assume that the rebels are protected by the night, the jungle, and the rain, and that technical means will deny this cover. The more fundamental protection of the rebels, however, comes from the support and involvement of millions of people on their side in what they call a people's war. The electronic battlefield, or any military program that operates with such a murderous and indiscriminate effect from the skies, can only unite more people in resistance against the US Air Force. The current winter–spring offensive in Laos and Cambodia demonstrates the failure of the sensors to stop the other side's ground operations, just as the master offensive during Tet in 1968 showed that military attacks could be secretly planned and carried out at 150 points in South Vietnam, including the American Embassy, virtually under the nose of the most sophisticated US intelligence staffs.

The bombing of North Vietnam from 1965–68 failed miserably, and the Pentagon Papers show that this judgment was shared by McNamara, the Defense Department intelligence desk, the CIA, and the Jason Division of the Institute for Defense Analysis.

Nevertheless, the Air Force and its various research and corporate contractors remain "optimistic" in spite of their failures. Despite the fact that their air war has been a scandal in its own terms, the most expensive exercise in futility ever devised, the Air Force always believes a few more bombs, gadgets, and new inventions will defeat the enemy. Now they claim that the "smart bombs" of the electronic battlefield are far more effective than those used in Operation Rolling Thunder over North Vietnam. They claim that the new technology cuts deeply into the Vietnamese ability to supply the fronts. In mid-December, 1971, Air Force Secretary Robert C.

Seamans held a press conference to extoll his new system. He claimed that of an estimated 68,500 tons of supplies the North Vietnamese sent down the Ho Chi Minh Trail during 1970–71, only 9,500 tons reached the intended fronts. Aside from the credibility of self-serving Air Force statistics, which never proved correct in the North Vietnam bombing campaign, *The New York Times* questioned why there was no indication of "ammunition shortages among the North Vietnamese troops fighting in Laos and Cambodia."

Testimony to the "success" of the Air Force strategy actually proves the opposite on close examination. Operation "Igloo White," the sensor-based campaign against the Ho Chi Minh Trail in 1970, was described in detail by General Evans to the Cannon Committee of the Senate. In response to Air Force interdiction, he said, the Vietnamese and Pathet Lao created "redundant lines of communication," an "elaborate road network," also increased the size of their truck fleet, and set up "more numerous heavier anti-aircraft defenses." It is also reported that after the Lam Son 719 fiasco in February, 1971, the other side *widened* the supply trail to three times its former width. The bombing simply cannot pinpoint the targets or penetrate the complex air defenses and bunkers of the Vietnamese, especially as their success on the ground broadens their potential field of operations. In addition to being triggered accidentally by water buffalo or other moving animals, the sensors apparently can be neutralized or avoided by the ground troops. The Vietnamese, for example, hang buckets of urine in treetops to draw fire into unpopulated areas. Instead of the "precision," the "surgical" capability the Air Force claims, a thrashing mad Frankenstein's monster has been loosed on Indochina.

Not only will this air war fail to subdue the enemy, it is going to deepen the problems of the Nixon government. First, the war can be escalated by the other side to neutralize the Air Force. Apparently during the offensive in northern Laos in late 1971, for example, the Pathet Lao troops were using new light antiaircraft weapons that could be carried in ground operations to offset the US air strikes. Secondly, the use of MIGs over Laos against slower-moving B52s was reported. By early 1971, the US had admitted the loss of about 8,000 aircraft, including 5,000 helicopters; the total cost of the fixed-wing craft was $4.4 billion, for helicopters $1.3 billion, a total loss of $5.7 billion. Figures like these were cited as a major problem in several of the Pentagon Papers documents.

Even more explosive a result of the air war will be the continued killing and capturing of US pilots. Although fewer in number than American ground losses, these dead and captured pilots have become a major political crisis for the Nixon Administration, partly because the Administration itself has made it a fundamental issue. During the sudden bombing raids of North Vietnam over Christmas, 1971, seven pilots were captured and two killed (from December 18–30), bringing the total held by North Vietnam to nearly 350, a number which will increase constantly.

So the real question is not whether the air war will succeed in its own terms, but whether it will be politically effective at home in buying time for Nixon in domestic politics. Will keeping the rebels at bay in Southeast Asia while lowering US ground casualties sufficiently placate or confuse public opinion in the United States?

Another question is whether all this destruction will be increased still further by an American escalation at any point that the Nixon Doctrine fails. Daniel Ellsberg and other past Pentagon advisers have suggested that the next US escalation target would be Hanoi or Haiphong harbor, but beyond that lies the even more evil prospect of atomic or nuclear weapons.

In this connection no less an authority than Clark Clifford was quoted, perhaps prophetically, in *The New York Times* of August 8, 1971:

> I think [Hanoi] will plan an offensive that will demonstrate to the American people that the war is not winding down, that it could go on forever, with high casualties among our residual force. My great concern is what Mr. Nixon's response might be. He might stop troop withdrawal. He might increase the bombing. He might reverse the withdrawal process and increase our troop strength. No one knows what he might do. We must remember that Mr. Nixon once said in a speech in Chicago that in modern warfare, tactical nuclear weapons must be considered conventional weapons.

A specific "final solution" to the problem of "infiltration" which might occur to Nixon is the use of atomic land mines. As described in the October 28, 1970, *The New York Times,* they sound intended for the Ho Chi Minh Trail or the DMZ:

> Atomic land mines could block a mountain pass against attacking forces by contaminating the areas with nuclear fallout and by caving in earth and rocks from the heights . . . in sparsely populated areas with relatively few avenues of invasion, atomic land mines could be an effective weapon.

In possible preparation for this atomic radiation belt, millions of people were removed from the area provinces immediately below the DMZ in 1971, to be relocated in the Mekong Delta or coastal highlands. As already pointed out, both Nixon and Kissinger have favored the use of atomic or nuclear weapons as a threat and, where necessary, actually used against America's adversaries. So have other highly important commentators and officials, specifically referring to the Vietnam war. In a November 15, 1971, *The New York Times* column, C. L. Sulzberger suggested that the "greatest lesson of the Vietnam war" is that limited conventional war is becoming "outmoded," while "total warfare is a dreadful absurdity." Therefore, a "third solution" might be in "the field of truly tactical atomic weapons." An even more ominous comment was made in the January, 1971, *Foreign Affairs* by Earl Ravenal, former director of the Asian Division in the Pentagon, in an article on "The Nixon Doctrine and Our Asian Commitments":

> Essentially we are to support the same level of potential involvement with smaller conventional forces. The specter of intervention will remain but the risk of defeat or stalemate will be greater; or *the nuclear threshold will be lower.*

Although a failure, the bombings have created a terrible slaughter and disruption. It is revealing that the Pentagon doesn't even keep figures, or have a category for, "civilian casualties." These unrecorded victims have not even the possibility of decent health care if they are only wounded. According to the Kennedy subcommittee on refugees, "Health services remain almost nonexistent" for the South Vietnamese people. There are only 1,000 Vietnamese doctors, nearly all of them assigned to the ARVN. The US AID budget for public health assistance has declined from even the inadequate figures of the late sixties. A 1970 Kennedy subcommittee summary pointed out that in South Vietnam "shortages of personnel and supplies remain acute," that it was "not uncommon to see two or three patients in a single bed, even in the model hospitals." For Laos, they reported overall hospital capacity to be "marginal," often hospitals at 200 percent of capacity, and "very severe shortages" of personnel and supplies. As for Cambodia there are no US funds at all for medical supplies and humanitarian relief. Investigators from the General Accounting Office (GAO) discovered that the US Embassy declined a request in June, 1971, from Cambodian officials for medical supplies. The US official suggested that the Cambodians seek aid from the Soviet Union, Japan, or Britain! The GAO Report, summarized in *The New York Times,* December 5, 1971, says: "The policy of the United States is *not to become involved with the problems of civilian war victims in Cambodia.*"

The human result of this neglect is thousands of unnecessary Asian deaths, while wounded American GIs are rushed to the most modern hospital facilities. The number of wounded GIs who die has dropped drastically with the new US treatment facilities, while helpless Vietnamese are left dying three to a bed for lack of doctors. In addition, among those "fortunate" enough to live, there is an incredible rate of amputation practiced because of the low level of medical facilities; and it is virtually impossible, without waiting for months and years, to obtain artificial limbs.

Somehow this is the most horrible part of the US policy, perhaps because of the evidence that lives are literally wasting away for lack of the simplest medical care, perhaps because it so utterly disproves America's claim to be interested in the welfare of the Vietnamese, and perhaps finally because of the absolute callous silence that prevails in the face of these crimes. I do not know of any Nixon major comments on refugees or civilian casualties, in his whole career, other than those famous "refugees from communism" in 1954. These were essentially Catholics and other Vietnamese who had sided with the French colonialists in a barbaric war and been defeated, running to the South to regroup and reestablish their privileges; many of them still fight today or profit from their relationship to the still-Catholic Thieu regime. American fanatics like Dr. Tom Dooley, with support from Vice President Nixon, called these people refugees from "the rim of hell," when in fact, they were more like pathetic traitors to their country. Yet today when the US has quite literally created a hell, a sea of fire and napalm and flying flechettes and bomblets which blow off human feet, the official word still is that the refugees of Indochina are fleeing from communist terror and crossing over to the Western side.

It is true, of course, that in a genuine guerrilla war there are few "civilians." Most people at least covertly support a side. But this does not justify the attitude which Father Carl Creswell, former Episcopal chaplain at Chu Lai, offered the Army's My Lai investigators: "as far as the US Army was concerned, there was no such thing as the murder of a Vietnamese civilian." Many people are noncombatants although their political views might support the insurgents. Those most likely to be injured or killed by bombing are not the actual liberation troops, who are well protected, but the exposed people of the villages and rice fields, and especially little children and old people. The number of *unarmed* people killed by the US has always been extremely high. At the My Lai massacre of unarmed villagers on March 16, 1968, for example, Task Force Barker initially reported "victory" over enemy troops, claiming 128 "VC" deaths but only *three* captured weapons.

Appalling approximations can be made to measure the scale of this problem which Nixon denies exists. Using information from the Kennedy subcommittee, Project Air War (which includes some former AID workers in Laos), and the GAO Report, a stark picture of civilian casualties emerges. These figures are conservative; for instance, they do not include the casualties of North Vietnam, where 29,000 civilian casualties in 1965–66 alone were estimated by the CIA in a Pentagon Papers document.

Richard Nixon is responsible, in less than three years, for killing, wounding, and making refugees of over four million people in a war which he claims to be winding down!

CIVILIAN CASUALTIES

I South Vietnam	1964–68	1969–August, 1971
Killed	235,000	100,000
Wounded	500,000	240,000
Refugees	4,245,300	1,450,000
Total	4,980,300	1,790,000

II Laos	1964–68	1969–August, 1971
Killed	50,000	50,000
Wounded	125,000	125,000
Refugees	500,000	500,000
Total	675,000	675,000

III Cambodia	1964–68	1969–August, 1971
Killed	(no figures)*	tens of thousands
Wounded	(no figures)*	tens of thousands
Refugees	(no figures)*	2,000,000
Total		2,020,000+

IV Totals 1964–August, 1971

Killed	445,000+
Wounded	1,000,000+
Refugees	8,695,300
Totals	10,140,300+

V Totals Killed, Wounded, Made Refugees

Under Johnson (1964–68)	5,655,300+
Under Nixon (1968–August, 1971)	4,485,000+

* No *official* bombing and no *official* casualties but several scores of Cambodians were killed in "accidental" US raids.

The Theory
of Forced Urbanization

All this disruption of life may seem aimless, insane, but actually there is a rationality to the whole process that makes it as deliberate a war crime as any that can be imagined. When the Air Force general made the infamous remark during the Tet Offensive that he "bombed the city to save it," he was speaking from an underlying philosophy that guides the American war effort at every level.

The destruction of the fabric of life in the liberated zones, the killing and displacing of so many people, is justified by the concept that it is all in their best interest. Their lives are thought to be backward, tradition-bound, and poor, lacking in middle-class possibilities altogether. Communism is said to feed on this backwardness; indeed, W. W. Rostow denounced it as the "scavenger" of the development process. The road to progress and a better life, even if it begins in a bombed village and then goes to a refugee camp, is the road to the city, to urbanization, to a world called "modern."

A name has been given to this process by one of those numerous intellectual servants of power, Samuel Huntington, former chairman of the Harvard government department and a regular adviser on Southeast Asia policy. Most theories of the Vietnam war, like counter-insurgency, came not from generals but from the Cambridge (liberal) complex: Harvard, Huntington, Kennedy. The names sound like a law firm; it becomes difficult to realize their doctrines are, legally speaking, crimes against humanity. Writing in *Foreign Affairs* of July, 1968, Huntington invented the phrase *"forced-draft urbanization."* Huntington describes the NLF as holding the "good Maoist expectation that by winning the support of the rural population it could eventually isolate and overwhelm the cities." And he says, ominously, the enemy will remain a "powerful force which cannot be dislodged from its constituency *so long as its constituency exists*."

But the NLF hasn't counted on the *"American-sponsored urban revolution"* brought about by the *"modernizing instruments of bombs and artillery"* which are "largely, if not exclusively" the cause of the "movement of the population into the cities."

> . . . if the "direct application of mechanical and conventional power" takes place on such a massive scale as to produce a massive migration from countryside to city, the basic assumptions underlying the Maoist doctrine of revolutionary warfare no longer operate. . . .
>
> In an absentminded way the United States may well have stumbled upon the answer to "wars of national liberation." The effective response lies neither in the quest for conventional military victory nor in the esoteric doctrines and gimmicks of counter-insurgency warfare. It is instead *forced-draft urbanization and modernization* which rapidly bring the country in question out of the phase in which a rural revolutionary movement can hope to generate sufficient strength to come to power.

It sounds so charming, this "absentminded" solution! It is difficult to realize this man is talking about the dislocation of over 9 *million* of the 27 million people of Laos, Cambodia, and South Vietnam. Just to be clear that Huntington is not making an isolated and embarrassing comment on the true meaning of US policy, the same views can be found coming from two top officials. The first, John Paul Vann, one of the highest-ranked US advisers in Vietnam: "We inadvertently stumbled on the solution to guerrilla warfare—urbanization" (*Newsweek,* January 20, 1969). The second, Robert Komer, the official in charge of pacification under Johnson:

> . . . at the low point of end-1964, only 40 percent of South Vietnam's population was under government "control"—

a sometime thing in those days . . . a high percentage in this increase in "relatively secure" population in 1965–67 (to 62 percent) *did not occur because of increased security in the countryside, but rather as a result of refugee movements and the accelerated urbanization taking place.*

This is yet another case of dull and dulling words masking an indescribably awful situation. Since 1962, Saigon's population has grown from 400,000 to four million; Danang, from 120,000 to 450,000; Hue from 104,000 to 200,000; Phnom Penh, from 600,000 in 1970 to two million in 1972; Vientiane, from 80,000 in 1968 to 160,000 in 1969, as Nixon doubled the bombing.

When John Kennedy came to office, South Vietnam was a 90 percent rural country; today it is 60 percent urban. Cambodia and Laos are going in the same direction faster.

Saigon was designed to accommodate 300,000 people by the French. Now there are over three million people within the twenty-one square miles of Saigon proper, and another million in bulging growths on the edge. It is the most densely populated city in the world, with approximately 150 persons per acre (Tokyo has 63 per acre). After 1966 there was not even room for squatters. In some cases, squatters had to be moved because their "homes" (little mats in the street) were blocking transportation. Once lovely shade trees are described now as "grotesque amputees." Garbage, never before a problem in Vietnam, has become an immediate hazard to life. The sewer system has collapsed, and the garbage-filled canals are no longer even dredged. Fully one fourth of the city's electricity is consumed by foreigners for air conditioning; several blackouts per week are ordinary. To the eyes of two American city planners, the city appears this way:

The squatters build their shelters from scraps of wood, metal, thatch, cardboard, and poles they have been able to buy, scavenge, or pilfer. The means of access in these settlements are labyrinths of narrow alleys about three feet in width. Mud, rancid cesspools, stagnant canals, rotting garbage, and human excrement make up the environment of the inhabitants. Around everything there is the constant buzz of flies. Empty artillery shells are used as stoves, and napalm containers are fabricated into family pots and pans. Periodically, fires sweep through these squalid settlements, wiping out forty to fifty shelters at a time. Fire-fighting facilities are too limited and ineffective to assist.

The Kennedy subcommittee described the degradation this way in 1968:

> They sleep in the alleys and the streets, in courtyards and halls, even in graveyards and mausoleums where bodies have been removed to allow more room. Most have no work. The children run wild; there is little food, little clothing to sustain them both physically and mentally. The areas they live in are breeding grounds for disease and illness and VC recruitment.

These shacks are better than the refugee camps that many of the Vietnamese were held in before coming to Saigon. It has been common for ten families to live in units built for one family in the camps. An average of thirteen persons were found to be living in one nine-by-fifteen-foot structure in a camp near Quang Ngai. The supplies to the camps are hopelessly inadequate, and 50 percent is siphoned into the black market anyway.

Health is the most shameful index of life in the camps and cities. Apart from the lack of aid for war victims, the level of unchecked disease in the cities is reflected in three facts: (1) One half of all Saigon's recorded deaths are children under five. (2) Bubonic plague has reappeared in Vietnam due to the garbage pits which breed deadly rats; from eight cases in 1961, the Saigon government reported an increase to 5,500 cases in 1967, and the figures are in fact much higher. (3) According to the World Health Organization, 60 percent of Saigon's people are infected with tuberculosis bacilli.*

All that this "modernizing" process represents, in fact, is a control program. There is not only no improvement in the standards of living for the migrants, but there is a terrible and threatening decline. Since nothing will be done to alleviate these conditions by Thieu and the US, what is happening is the creation of an explosive mass in the cities. This is the ironic opposite of Huntington's thesis. Instead of eroding, the base of revolution has been compressed and moved closer to the institutional centers of power in the cities. The Tet Offensive proved the widespread existence of resistance organizations inside all the urban areas, and proved the inability of the US–Saigon police to control or apprehend urban revolutionaries any more than they were able to control the guerrillas in the countryside. The number of anti-American demonstrations and "incidents" in the cities has increased each year, with Americans being kept behind barbed wire or permanently on base in many places. American cars are frequently burned, and individuals attacked in the streets when they go out. With typical wide-eyed innocence one reporter commented in 1971 that:

> Americans involved in traffic accidents with the South Vietnamese, regardless of whose fault it is, often find themselves surrounded by crowds of angry and fist-waving Vietnamese. . . .

* This fact is not necessarily alarming to American officials and military men who spend time in Saigon's brothels, as they would rather have a prostitute with tuberculosis than one with syphilis. One commonly hears male banter like this: "Didn't she cough? You shouldn't fuck her if she doesn't cough."

Plans for the Americanization
of Vietnamese Economics,
Politics, and Culture

American plans for the Vietnamese do not end with depositing them in the congested cities. For the Vietnamese who have been driven into the US-controlled zones, a new system of domination awaits them: a growing Western-oriented consumer market economy.

As early as March, 1966, *Fortune* was claiming that "a South Vietnam preserved from communism has the potential to become one of the richest nations in Southeast Asia":

> It is not a bit too early for the US, which has sent some of its finest military minds to the Vietnam war, to send eminent experts on agriculture, transportation, education, and industry to prepare plans for South Vietnam's postwar economic development.

Almost on signal, this is what has happened. Japanese and American corporations are moving rapidly into South Vietnam. Economists and technicians are studying the economy, its natural resources, manpower supply, and quality of labor force, and drafting plans for the future. Even though investment is a high-risk proposition because of the war, and even though (as one planner says) *"the Anglo-American concept of the corporation has not made much headway,"* the official plans are piling up, which point *not so much to an American withdrawal but to at least a decade of economic Westernization.*

The reports which provide the basis for this conclusion are: *The Postwar Development of the Republic of Vietnam,* a joint US–Saigon study directed by David Lilienthal (former New Deal head of TVA) for President Johnson, completed and presented to Nixon in early 1969; RAND Corporation reviews of the Lilienthal Report; a several-volume study entitled *Southeast Asia's Economy in the Seventies,* done in November, 1970, for the US-controlled Asian Development Bank in Manila; economic projections by Columbia University economist Emile Benoit, published as part of the Asian Development Bank study; an economic report on South Vietnam for the Institute for Defense Analysis (a branch of the Pentagon) by Arthur Smithies of the CIA, RAND, and formerly of the US Budget Bureau; a study, connected to Lilienthal's, by Japanese economist Masataka Ohta for Japan's Federation of Economic Organizations; another by Smithies, with Allan Goodman, another RAND consultant, on "The Possible Role of the United Nations and Other International Organizations in the Economic Rehabilitation of Vietnam," on a 1971 State Department grant to Columbia University; and various articles appearing in journals like *Fortune* and *Le Monde.*

These reports are all official in the sense that they were done as advisory studies for the US, Japanese, or Saigon governments. What they say is not necessarily reflected in policy, but they certainly shape or influence final policy. None of them are secret, although as little publicity as possible seems to be given them by either the government or the press. What is most significant about them as a whole is the general insight they give into US plans for the future of Vietnam and the arrogant way in which US officials and planners think about their roles.

The reports, to begin with, make it clear that the South Vietnamese economy on which the US hopes to build is now a catastrophe. The roots of catastrophe lie in the fact that the economy is entirely artificial, a creation of American military, economic, and political institutions. This economic artificiality parallels the military artificiality of the ARVN, and both stem originally from the diplomatic artificiality of the South

Vietnamese "state" itself, which was devised by the 1954 Geneva Conference as a temporary state but transformed into an American protectorate immediately afterwards.

The symptoms of the Saigon economic crisis are several:

1. *Manpower* is absorbed almost entirely in US-sponsored sectors. The largest of these, of course, is the military. South Vietnam has the fourth largest army in the "free world," absorbing over one million men, requiring 70 percent of its national budget. Only 3 percent of the entire work force is employed in local industry.

2. *Inflation* is epidemic, the consumer price index rising astronomically every year. Asian Development Bank figures show a 17 percent rise in 1965, 62 percent in 1966, 44 percent in 1967, 28 percent in 1968, 21 percent in 1969, a projected 30 percent for 1970. South Vietnamese inflation was ranked the worst of fifty countries surveyed by *Business Week* in its October 24, 1970, issue.

3. *Corruption* infects the economy at every level. Arthur Smithies grants it is "generally acknowledged that Vietnam is corrupt" and in his report concludes this "may be irreversible."

4. *Taxes* of an adequate nature are beyond Saigon's ability to collect from its own population. The Asian Development Bank study estimates a 1970 inflow of 100 billion piastres to Saigon, half in economic aid and half in US defense spending, but the Saigon government is only able to collect 110 billion piastres in revenues—fully 70 billion of which are derived from imports, not taxes.

5. *Imports* are the basis of the economy. Because of the war, and Japanese and American imports, South Vietnam has lost its export capacity almost completely. *The New York Times* 1972 Economic Review for Asia, January 24, 1972, in an article smartly titled "Withdrawal Pains," estimates that imports outweigh exports by a *100:1 ratio*. The clearest ex-

ample is rice. Once the "rice bowl" of Southeast Asia, South Vietnam is now utterly dependent on the United States for its rice supply. From an export level of 250,000 tons in 1959, South Vietnam had fallen to a point of importing 850,000 tons by 1968. The same pattern is occurring with the rubber crop: from $44 million worth of exports in 1961, the level fell to $9 million in 1969. An ADB report estimates that manufacturing has collapsed to one half of what it was in the early sixties, "vividly illustrating the shift from domestic production to imports." The collapse has been as swift as it has been drastic: from 1965 to 1969, imports rose from $250 million to nearly $800 million worth of goods, while total exports fell from a slender $40 million to an infinitesimal $15 million. A remarkable illustration of the artificiality is that by 1969, the real value of imports equaled the entire South Vietnamese Gross National Product! In other words, Nixon began "Vietnamization" with a 100 percent dependent economy.

US aid in the decade of the sixties totalled $16.5 billion to South Vietnam. Economic aid rose from $146 million in 1961 to $614 million in 1970; military aid from $65 million to $1.9 billion annually in the same period. The overall totals are $4 billion of economic assistance, $7.75 billion of military, and about $5 billion for related infrastructure costs.

It is important to remember that South Vietnam's fate is a "model" for Cambodia, Laos, South Korea, Thailand, and the Philippines. The two most decayed are Cambodia, whose rice and rubber exports have also collapsed, and who now depends on $300 million in annual US aid, and Laos, which has already been described as the country most dependent on the US in the world. The crisis of South Vietnam, in short, is the crisis of all of America's dependencies throughout the Pacific Basin.

Yet the same reports which contain this evidence of catastrophe outline a bright future for South Vietnam through a series of fantastic projections. The war, it turns out, has been progressive for the people of South Vietnam, though somewhat damaging, for it has now placed them in the takeoff stage just prior to prosperity and happiness. All the maimed and widows and orphans should be reassured with these prospects:

> Southeast Asia can expect to enjoy rapid economic growth through export expansion provided she pursues economic policies to link up her abundant national resources with the expanding world market demand for their products. (*Asian Development Bank*)
>
> Physical destruction is minimal . . . and the economic wealth of the country has increased. . . . It is true that large numbers of citizens have been displaced from their homes, but others have acquired new skills which will be valuable to the growing economy. (*Lilienthal Report*)
>
> [the Mekong Delta] is the most valuable piece of real estate in the world. (*Lilienthal to the press, 1968*)
>
> The war has changed the situation in ways which are distinctly favorable to development. (*Arthur Smithies*)

As the imagination wonders at the twisted optimism of these statements and struggles to understand what they mean, at least two possibilities appear.

First, the physical infrastructure created by the war is now "the best in Southeast Asia" according to *Fortune* (if for no other reason, one realizes, than that North Vietnam's infrastructure has been so heavily bombed). American planners glow at the thought of the 2,400 miles of highway, the countless bridges, the 600 miles of railroad line, the 200 airfields (five large enough for passenger jets), and the six major ports which have been built in the ruins of South Vietnam.

Second, the growth of a cheap and relatively skilled labor force "trained in the basic routines of industrial life" excites the planners. This is a "social infrastructure." The Japanese business study analyzes the South Vietnamese people "from the viewpoint of labor quality," and finds them "superior to the inhabitants of adjacent nations." The report stresses "ensuring an adequate supply of high-quality and inexpensive labor, which does not quit easily." This "supply of cheap labor" is "without a doubt . . . the greatest attraction for foreign interests in investing in Vietnam." And to ADB planners, cheap labor is also the "chief attraction for the international manufacturing corporations seeking to find suitable locations for their component industries." Smithies urges that South Vietnamese wages continue to be held down as an incentive for foreign investment.

South Vietnam is to fulfill a specific role in the vast regional economy dominated by the US which has been called the Pacific Rim. The president of the Bank of America, Rudolph Peterson, defined this area in *California Business,* September–October, 1968:

> When I speak of the Pacific Rim, I am putting the broadest possible construction on the term—the western coasts of South America, Central America and our own continent, and extending beyond Australia and the Far East to India. There is no more vast or rich area for resource development or trade growth in the world today than this immense region, and *it is virtually our own front yard.* . . .
>
> I emphasize that this is a largely underdeveloped area, yet an area rich in an immense variety of resources and potential capabilities. Were we California businessmen to play a more dynamic role in helping trade development in the Pacific Rim, we would have *giant, hungry new markets for our products and vast new profit potentials for our firms.*

The importance of these potential "hungry new markets" to the American capitalist economy is great. In the year before Nixon took office, the Vietnam war came to a crisis simultaneously with a crisis of American trade. After dominating its global market network for years, the US began to show a trade deficit. Other countries, notably Japan, were becoming able to export their goods more competitively than American firms. Faced with this impasse, the only answer traditionally has been to find new areas of expansion, new markets to serve as outlets for US goods or countries where American firms can be based less expensively because of cheaper labor costs and tax concessions. Although the US trades and invests primarily with Western Europe and Canada, its trade tends to be increasing more rapidly with the Pacific countries than with Europe, and the *potential* trade with Pacific countries is virtually untapped in comparison with Europe.

The US relies mainly on Japan as its economic partner in the Pacific, and increasingly since Nixon's announcement of the Guam Doctrine. But Japan is not "safely" in the American economic orbit, even though US oil companies dominate Japan's vital flow of oil for production. Japan is an overcrowded island with enormous needs for both foodstuffs and natural resources which can only be supplied through trade. This is one of the vital roles of Vietnam and all of Indochina, as Dwight Eisenhower claimed long ago. He called Indochina the region which

> Japan must have as a trading area, or it would force Japan to turn toward China and Manchuria, or toward the communist areas in order to live. The possible consequences of the loss of Japan to the free world are just incalculable.

Nixon as Vice President echoed Ike faithfully in 1954:

> If this whole part of Southeast Asia goes under communist domination or communist influence, Japan, who trades and must trade with this area in order to exist, must inevitably be oriented toward the communist regime.

The Stanford Research Institute, which does research for both the US government and the companies involved in the

Pacific Rim, declared in 1967 that the Vietnam war *"must be viewed as a struggle likely to determine the economic as well as the political future of the whole region."*

South Vietnam's role is to be a vital subarea in what Asian Development Bank calls a "new international division of labor." Its economic roles would be (1) to continue as a market for US investments; (2) to be a purchasing point for subsidiary companies to obtain goods from the US; (3) to supply rice, lumber, rubber, and other goods to countries like Japan. Its own manufacturing responsibility, in the words of the ADB, would be the *"production of components for multinational companies which [would then] assume the responsibility for world marketing of the output."* Electronic parts, bicycle and motorcycle components are specifically mentioned as products.

Thus even before the war ends, the US is shaping a new economic system in which the Vietnamese people are supposed to play a vital but subordinate role, and in which their economy and national independence will be in the hands of the US and Japan.

Smithies is one of the main strategists of this new international economic arrangement. His IDA paper calls for a "consortium" of countries like the US, Japan, Australia, Thailand, New Zealand, Korea, and the Philippines, "but the *club* should not be exclusive." The Asian Development Bank should administer development assistance, and so too will the World Bank which "has already begun to cooperate with the UN in the Mekong." (Robert McNamara heads this institution, a clear illustration of the way bombing and "aid" are two sides of the same coin, made in America.) The International Monetary Fund, the World Health Organization, the United Nations Special Fund also are enlisted, although Smithies concludes there are certain limits: it would be "premature for international organizations to promote higher labor or welfare standards [in Vietnam] in the immediate future." All these bodies are considered in the more authoritative Smithies–Goodman study for the State Department, which seeks to create an international, or at least multilateral cover for what is obviously intended to be continued US penetration.

Private enterprise, and especially foreign private investment, are central to the American plans. Apparently the Saigon government has not been pliant enough to suit all the needs of private businessmen, so the reports suggest various revisions of the South Vietnamese legal system. In a modest understatement, for instance, Lilienthal points out that

> Understandably, after twenty years of war, during which large numbers of foreigners have become prominent and influential in the country, various forms of xenophobia have appeared [meaning a nationalistic preference for the public sector and direct controls].

Ambassador Bunker has worked effectively to smooth out any laws which might stand in the way of foreign investment. Speaking before the US Chamber of Commerce, Saigon branch, in February, 1971, he announced plans for

> . . . *an effective strategy to further participation in foreign trade and to attract private investment from abroad* . . . the recent petroleum law and the new investment law now before the upper house indicate the government's desire to create a flexible long-term investment policy which will serve Vietnam's interests while at the same time create an *economic climate foreign investors will find attractive.*

Into this friendly environment American banks and both Japanese and American investors have come in rising numbers. Banking, the key to credit and investment, will basically be under US control. As far back as 1966 a vice president of the First National City Bank had this positive view of the future:

We believe that we're going to win this war. Afterwards you'll have a major job of reconstruction on your hands. That will take financing and financing means banks. It would be illogical to permit the English and French to monopolize the banking business because South Vietnam's economy is becoming more and more United States-oriented.

American corporations like Standard Oil, Shell, and Ford have moved into South Vietnam, and dozens of other contractors, builders, machine tool companies, and producers of agricultural equipment are involved. Alongside them are the expanding Japanese business interests: farm machinery factories, telephone and water works systems, a Sony assembly plant; and Toyota is rumored to be coming. Japanese business investment in Saigon was only $4 million from 1960–69, but since the Nixon Doctrine, Japanese investment has jumped to $32 million. "As the Americans withdraw, the Japanese are becoming more visible here," reported *The New York Times,* December 12, 1971. Motorcycles, televisions, radios, rice cookers, fans, refrigerators, and phonographs—all Japanese-made —"are all commonly found in Vietnamese middle-class homes."

In the rural areas, the key to private growth of the economy is the heralded "green revolution," which means the use of so-called miracle-grain rice and fertilizers to increase the output of rice by the remaining peasantry. This program is crucial to the reversal of the imports problem and the unemployment problem. Rice must become a major export item once again, and only the development of the "green revolution" can provide options to urban unemployment. Lilienthal's assistant, Nicholas Philip, sees the "green revolution" additionally as a major opportunity for American investors. New storage dams, flood control levees, irrigation and drainage canals, and pumping stations will be required, all built by American contractors and financed by American banks (credit will be crucial for obtaining seed, fertilizers, and the necessary equipment). "It is in these areas," Philip advises, "in addition to agricultural production, that *greatly expanded opportunities for private investment in support of agricultural development can occur.*" The corollary is a further increase in the centralization of land-holdings, for it is impossible to obtain the credit and operate efficiently otherwise. Robert Komer, America's pacification director, spoke in 1969 of the 3,400 tractors being used in the Delta, twice as many as in 1964, as the key to making (some) Delta farmers "the new rich" in Vietnam. Emile Benoit of Columbia takes it for granted that there should be "centralization of decision-making in the most competent hands."

To theorists like Lilienthal and Philip, the traditional Vietnamese farmer stands unknowingly in the way of his own progress. They criticize the "parochialism" of the peasant who is sadly "content with subsistence farming" and "wants to work his own little plot of land," for "that is not practical if there is to be a big boom in rice production." These farmers should look forward to becoming part of "an efficient farm labor force," the Lilienthal Report concludes.

There is considerable controversy within the planning establishment about the "green revolution" and land reform. Even the authors of the Asian Development Bank report on the "green revolution" are more troubled than Lilienthal. They point out that centralizing and mechanizing agriculture will add to the problem of displaced labor. "If productive uses are found for the land and labor, and if methods are devised for cushioning the accelerated degree of dislocation entailed," they think the rural program can succeed without accentuating the "problems of unemployment and disadvantaged farmers."

Lilienthal and certain RAND Corporation economists have insisted that land reform is not the crucial issue it is supposed to be in winning the peasantry. They are criticized

[65]

heavily by Robert L. Sansom in a little-studied volume called *The Economics of Insurgency in the Mekong Delta*. A member of the National Security Council staff, Sansom is frank about conceding the real improvements brought to rural people's lives under the NLF land-reform program. He grants that the American-sponsored "land reform" under Diem was fake, and that "eight million of the Delta's ten million people received economic benefits from Viet Cong land-reform measures" through the early sixties. He criticizes US planners for refusing "to credit the Viet Cong with the considerable social and economic benefits" they provided the people. "The Americans offered the peasant a constitution; the Viet Cong offered him his land and with it the right to survive," he rightly says.

But Sansom, in his stress on the importance of real land reform, is no NLF partisan. On the contrary, he cynically believes in wiping out the communists regardless of what progress they have achieved in the countryside. His frankness turns into the usual "pentagonese" in describing how the American bombing from 1965 on has eroded the gains made in the countryside by the NLF. Interviews with peasants show that "security was the overriding condition" in making them leave NLF areas and move into Saigon-controlled ones. What this in fact means is that the United States intervened massively in 1965 not only against an NLF army which was on the verge of taking power in Saigon, but intervened as well against a successful NLF organization which was improving the standard of living in the countryside.

The sophisticated way to erode the base of the NLF, to Sansom, is not through bombing, but through dealing with the grievances of the small farmers, and here he turns to the "green revolution" and its technology. He advocates that aid should flow even into NLF-controlled areas—"fertilizers, motor pumps, tractors, land reform, and the like"—all of which will lessen support for the insurgents by lessening grievances, and ultimately by making the people in the NLF zones dependent on Western technology and the market system which supplies it.

The potentially most important questions about economic exploitation of South Vietnam and Indochina, however, revolve about neither countryside nor city but about the vast stretches of the South China Sea—where *oil* is said to lie in abundance. With the greedy excitement of the British seeking ivory in Africa and the Americans seeking gold in California, US oil companies are becoming involved in Southeast Asia. There have been persistent reports of secret negotiations between the State Department, the Saigon government, and the oil companies. Although all sides now minimize the oil issue because of public protest ("You won't find anyone here willing to talk about it and be identified. It's become a real hot potato," said one oilman in the April, 1971, *Journal of Commerce*), there is undeniable evidence of the growing "oil stake" in Vietnam.

In 1969 initial explorations off South Vietnam's coast were begun by Ray Geophysical, in cooperation with Saigon, and representing "an unidentified group of US and foreign oil companies." In the same year, a petroleum development law favorable to foreign investors was passed in Saigon.

In May, 1970, David Rockefeller predicted $35 billion would be invested by oil companies in Asia, especially Southeast Asia, over the next twelve years. That same spring the *US Journal of Commerce* declared that South Vietnam "may contain the richest petroleum deposits in Southeast Asia. And the influential *Petroleum Engineer* in June, 1970, tied the oil issue to a satisfactory settlement in Vietnam:

> If and when the US wins its objectives there, oil exploration conceivably could be successful enough to turn that part of the world into another south Louisiana–Texas type producing area. This would be one of the biggest booms in the industry's history. It all depends on the Vietnam war, how long it takes to get the job done and how well the job is done.

The discovery of oil could salvage the economic situation in South Vietnam, or so the US planners hope. Smithies says "the outlook for the future will be transformed if oil is discovered," and *The New York Times* 1971 Asian economic report sees the "greatest hope" for increasing Saigon's exports in "the possibility that oil beds lying offshore will turn out to be exploitable commercial ventures."

Not only is oil crucial for rescuing South Vietnam, however; it is imperative for the American empire as a whole. Economist Malcolm Caldwell estimates that America, Western Europe, and Japan are the "most precariously placed consumer regions of all" in the global scramble for energy sources. The US imports one fourth of its oil from abroad, its greatest import need; fully a third of US private investment abroad is in oil. This voracious appetite for oil is increasing; already as much as 40 percent of the American Gross National Product is dependent on the oil supply. The big oil companies (thirty-three of them account for one third of the total joint earnings of *Fortune*'s top five hundred corporations) demand and require "stability" for their investments in oil-rich regions where enormous amounts of private capital are required for exploration alone. This "stability" must be provided by the US government, by military means if necessary. Has the Nixon government already promised this "stability" to the oil companies in South Vietnam? Gulf, which now has an arrangement with Japan, has replied to a Congressman's inquiry about South Vietnam with: "We are obliged to play our cards close to our chest . . . so far as our future plans are concerned."

The evidence dictates the conclusion that the US, instead of withdrawing, is constantly probing and deepening new interests in Indochina. The only question is the degree. The cost figures, for example, vary. The Lilienthal Report proposed $2.5 billion of direct military and economic aid to Saigon for the decade ahead. RAND's Albert Williams, writing after the Tet Offensive, criticized Lilienthal's figure for being too low. Williams suggested twice as much for ten years. Williams also cautions against a negotiated settlement and advocates a policy "not very different from the present one" as being best for insuring foreign investment.

Emile Benoit goes beyond all these figures to propose in the Asian Development Bank report a total of *$13 billion* in economic and military assistance for only a *five-year period, 1970–75.* This amount, $9 billion of which would be military aid, would nearly equal the entire US investment of $16.5 billion for the whole decade of the sixties.

Who has informed the American people that after spending more than $100 billion to win the Vietnam war so far, they are about to support a rotten Saigon dictatorship for another ten years?

Though these economic plans provide the main basis for continued American intervention, control of the political life of South Vietnam is not left to chance either. All the economic investment and projections could be threatened at any moment by the collapse of the Thieu dictatorship (or whatever pro-US clique is in power). Therefore the US has been continually involved in the manipulation of Saigon politics, from the moment the Catholic reactionary Ngo Dinh Diem was fostered in 1954 until the present time. Of the many documents revealing the nature of US political penetration, the most striking in several ways is, again, by Harvard's Samuel Huntington.*

* Huntington appears to be among the most important and least known of the various intellectual advisers who have given direction to the criminal US effort in Vietnam. In addition to his doctrines of "forced urbanization" and political manipulation, this government professor takes an active interest in direct military affairs. An important overview, titled *Counter-Insurgency Warfare,* by Air Force Major John S. Pustay, carries a jacket blurb by Huntington praising it as a "systematic, analytical handbook" filling a "real need in guerrilla warfare literature." Of those intellectuals who have kept a university cover instead of entering government service directly, Huntington seems to be at the top.

"Getting Ready for Political Competition in South Vietnam" is the title of Huntington's sweeping document. It was presented in March, 1969, to the Southeast Asia Development Advisory Group (SEADAG), a policy-developing arm of the Asia Society (CIA funded) and the official US Agency for International Development (AID). The paper may be a response to his Harvard associate Kissinger's lament on the lack of a "political corollary" to US military power in the South; all that Huntington admits, in a discreet footnote, is that the document is based on "brief talks with perhaps a dozen Washington officials" and "casual reference to a few documents."

To begin with, Huntington complains that "much of our grief" in Vietnam stems from "not becoming deeply enough involved" in that country's politics during the late fifties (when insurgency began) and immediately after Diem's fall in 1963 (when coup followed coup in Saigon). Since early 1966, however, he takes pride in the "active role" of the US in seeking a "viable political system."

The first task of political competition is to "get the opponent to agree to play the game," then "beat him at the game" —in other words, develop a rigged political system and force your opponent to accept it.

American bombing is the force Huntington counts on, not only for "forced urbanization" but for getting the NLF to play the game of politics. He is, of course, more euphemistic; the bombing is "inducing substantial migration." And then more matter of factly: "The NLF's principal incentive to engage in political competition is the beating it is getting in the military competition."

The future of Vietnam "lies in its cities," of course, so the key to a successful political deal is to offer the NLF the countryside in exchange for US control of the cities and trade. The NLF will thus have some semi-autonomous zones temporarily, but the immediate price will be acceptance of the "formal authority" of the Saigon government, thus reducing the NLF in status to that of a sect rather than a force bidding for national power.

The NLF will also have to allow the "free movement and security of goods and commerce" through their districts, much in the way envisioned by Sansom in his Mekong Delta study. With pro-American elements controlling the Saigon ministries of agriculture, health, and education, the new "national economy" will "eventually undermine the NLF power base."

In the usual cynical vein, Huntington concedes the NLF has done a better job than Saigon in bridging the gap between countryside and city with a rural–urban revolutionary movement, but all this can be reversed with US power which will both "induce substantial migration" and "promote economic development in rural areas and marketing and transportation links between them and the cities." If the NLF boycotts this policy, they will lose popular support as living standards begin to rise in the cities; if, on the other hand, the NLF integrates into the process, the local grievances they build upon will be "undermined by economic development and *the opportunities for entrepreneurship* opened up by the integration of these areas into the national economy."

Next there is the problem of rigging the political structure. "The electoral system," the professor informs us, has to be "compatible with the interests of the dominant groups." The problem is that the NLF is the most politically cohesive force in South Vietnam, he admits, and the urban areas can become "the principal source of opposition to the government." The US–Saigon side is weak, he says, because of the "personalistic individualism" and "absence of trust in social behavior." One might ask just what has caused the US to align with and foster such Vietnamese when clearly the "other" Vietnamese, those in the resistance, are unburdened by such difficult qualities. But not Huntington. He is obsessed with the "low level of political modernization" and the danger of a "politics of factionalism." He is fallen, one supposes in an "absentminded way" again, into the political scientist's great dream, of reliving the creation of the American government, when he compares Vietnam's factional woes to those of eighteenth-century America.

He looks favorably on the Catholic minority in Saigon which in 1967 was able, with only 10 percent of the population, to elect 43 percent of the Saigon Senate. The best way to duplicate this kind of "democracy" in the face of NLF opposition, he proposes, is through a "majority runoff" system. This would allow the "personalistic individualism" of the primary to be checked in a two-person runoff, and "covert" payoffs and "pork-barrel projects" can be used to induce the losers to unite against the NLF candidate.

As if this was not enough, Huntington proposes the US create its own opposition to the government which it supports in Saigon—just so that the NLF won't be able to monopolize the urban opposition. He proposes going to Generals Thi and Minh, and to the Buddhist Thich Tri Quang and suggesting they "take the lead in organizing the urban opposition."

He also urges even more horrible alternatives for the victimized masses of forced urbanization. The disintegrating culture of the cities should give rise to "messianic leaders," perhaps the reemergence of Buddhist sectarianism, possibly a fanatic cult like the Japanese Sokka Gakkai (because of the "prominent role which Japanese interests may play in postwar reconstruction"), or an Argentine-style Peronist movement: any of these "ought to be viewed favorably from the US–GVN viewpoint."

Huntington's paper, like the economic reports, seems to be one part fantasy, one part failure, one part reality. The fantasy, of course, comes from the massive arrogance which assumes everything and everyone can be rigged so easily. The

NLF has not been "induced" into playing the game; the US has failed to capture the urban population because the "US-sponsored urban revolution" has driven the South Vietnamese into deep anti-Americanism. The Huntington plan is a failure because it was designed in 1969 to create at least the image of a broader political spectrum in Saigon politics. But instead Thieu turned aside any proposals for such "broadening" in the ruthlessly managed 1971 election when he ran unopposed (Why should Thieu, who no doubt is aware of schemes like Huntington's, cooperate with the Americans in building an opposition which might replace him?). Finally the Huntington plan has a certain reality because it reflects the routine and relentless thinking which American policy makers are constantly engaged in as they try to salvage their interests in Vietnam. Because the plan is fantastic, and met with failure in 1971, does not mean that these planners will stop in their attempts to translate their fantasies into reality at the continued expense of the Vietnamese people. The plan has a pedagogical reality also because the scheme to create an opposition shows how empty are the dreams of many American liberals for a "third force" between Thieu and the NLF. That "third force" would be an American front, created behind the scenes.

A very crucial assumption behind this US strategy, which all the economists and planners seem to share, is that an American victory, or at least a continuing US presence, will result from the war. Lilienthal, who submitted his three-volume report to Nixon in early 1969, presumed a two- or three-year postwar construction period followed by a ten-year "development period," Smithies says the "best planning assumptions" seem to be a "military stalemate" and a "withering away of the war, a process that can last for a decade or more." The Japanese study, which proposes that economic penetration should intensify even before the war ends, predicts two years to reconstruct Vietnam, four to six years to build a new economy. Benoit shows how mechanical the planning mentality is when he hypothesizes that in 1973 "Hanoi will be forced to abandon its military effort either permanently or for the rest of the decade." This assumption is necessary, he writes, because

> (a) the consequences if Hanoi wins are nearly unpredictable; and
>
> (b) the problems of Vietnam would not, in such a case, be of concern to the Ministerial Conference for Economic Development of Southeast Asia and to the Asian Development Bank, since it is most unlikely that Vietnam would then remain a member.

In these lines by Benoit is the perfect example of how a "model" or hypothesis begins to take on a completely undeserved reality. It should be denounced simply for being abstract, were it not that such reports, as *Fortune* proposed in 1966, are partly designed to "be an important psychological weapon against the Viet Cong" by setting plans in motion for the continuance of US intervention. Little wonder that the Vietnamese should express suspicion about America's stated intentions in Vietnam: American negotiators' promises of "withdrawal" and "self-determination" stand contradicted as meaningless alongside these economic plans, as does America's pious interest in an "independent South Vietnam."

When we recall that such planning goes back to 1956 when US propagandists were proclaiming the "economic miracle" of South Vietnam, we see the way these seemingly unreal reports form a crucial part of the justification and guidance for the ongoing US machinery in Indochina. While the assumption of economic miracles or winning the war by 1973 is as much a fantasy as all previous victory claims of this generation, another assumption of these economic reports has a more ominous and corrosive present reality for the people of Vietnam. A root assumption is that a *cultural* transformation in the attitudes and psyches of the people of South Vietnam can be wrought by the introduction of the American market system and material values there.

The economic and political reports speak of the backwardness of the people which American industry can help them overcome: Smithies sees the necessity for attitudes of "industry" rather than "idleness" to develop in the Vietnamese character. He sums up the process in one statement:

> *A Honda-riding generation may be more capable of economic development than a buffalo-driving one.*

A common attitude among American planners is that of V. L. Elliot: *"we can WHAM [Win Hearts And Minds] the Vietnamese with our Hondas and motor pumps";* among military men it is "get all Vietnamese males on a Honda and the war will end." A million of the Honda motorbikes, in fact, are said to have been imported to Saigon in the last four years.

The October, 1971, issue of *Fortune* states the long-run perspective, as usual, in a class-conscious way:

> In the end, perhaps the most important legacy of US involvement in Vietnam will be the *introduction of modern industrial organization. Exposure to Western ideas and technology has profoundly changed traditional Vietnamese attitudes. More than highways or ports, these trained people could be the most valuable part of the new infrastructure being left behind in Vietnam by the US.*

These statements mean essentially that the people driven into the cities as refugees will be absorbed into a materialistic value system, will become turned on to Sony transistor radios and Honda motorbikes, to the whole Western consumer culture, and therefore leave behind their traditional and communist ways. In the process, the basis of their national identity and ability will be eroded. North Vietnam's leading poet To Huu has said the American target in South Vietnam is not simply military slaughter but "the poisoning of people's souls."

The process is already under way, at least among a minority in the cities. Shaplen says the Vietnamese have been bitten by the "bug of the affluent society," citing the thousands of television antennas sticking up among the shacks of Saigon. In the degrading bar culture of Saigon there are 400,000 registered prostitutes, who not only are separated from their families and cultural ways but also face a hopeless future of drugs and suicide. The family, which is Vietnam's most hallowed institution, is inevitably being shredded in this process, and with it much of the cultural underpinning of society. There are at least 250,000 orphans of GIs in South Vietnam, according to the most conservative figures. In one day in December, 1969, fifteen teen-agers committed suicide.

The cultural degradation of America's Saigon allies may be measured by the thousands of "beautifying" operations given each month to change the eyelids, noses, chins, and breasts of South Vietnamese women. About 40 percent of the operations are performed on "bar girls who cater to American clientele," according to one investigation reported in the *Los Angeles Times* of February 29, 1972. The rest are performed on "members of Vietnamese high society," including the wives of Thieu and Ky who both underwent eye operations several years ago. Mrs. Ngo Van Hieu, the reputed Jackie Kennedy of the Cantho district, whose clinic performs 1,000 operations per month, explains that the sexual standards of *Playboy* magazine have taken root in her circles. Historically "American and Vietnamese conceptions are completely different," Mrs. Hieu acknowledged. Before, Vietnamese didn't place so much importance on the body and people thought a little girl had the ideal form. But during the last thirty years and particularly in the last ten years the Vietnamese have begun to pay more attention to the body." The clinic's three surgeons are ARVN doctors who received their medical training in the United States. One of them, Mrs. Hieu's brother, is a deputy in the

Saigon Assembly. The clinic charges $120 for an eye operation and up to $480 for breast surgery "depending upon the size of the patient's original bust." In addition, the clinic performs ten to fifteen free operations per month on war victims. Mrs. Hieu's late husband, a deputy in the Assembly from Cantho, founded the clinic. He "was killed by terrorists," she claims, "for political reasons."

The NLF and various nationalist organizations struggle directly against this cultural degradation. The NLF slogan is that "there are more bars and brothels than hospitals, more prisons than schools" (the same line taken by the Pathet Lao against a similar situation).

The Americans, on the other hand, deliberately encourage these trends—as Huntington points out, they are in the US "interest." Vietnamization turns out to be Americanization. The effect of US policy is to create in mind and body a new subservient upper class in Vietnam. More fundamental than the eye operations is the surgery performed on the Vietnamese national consciousness. Two examples can make this clear. First, the CIA funds a literary magazine in Saigon, which is one of many ways an "existentialist" philosophy of accommodation to this hideous reality is propagated. In a recent number, a short story contains this bit of consoling advice:

> What is happiness? No such thing exists. Only acceptance is real. To accept, that's all.

A second example is the Vietnamese-American Association, a US-supported educational institution which trains bar girls and the Saigon civil service in the English language in "Americana." President Thieu attended the school, and its director, Daniel J. Herget says, "You can pick almost any man in government. At one time or another most of them have been through here." (*Los Angeles Times,* March 12, 1972.) Many of the school's 16,000 students "work for American firms and see English as the language of the future in South Vietnam."

These "well-mannered" students, according to the *Los Angeles Times,* "would warm the heart of any American president beset by generation troubles."

The same degeneracy is being introduced in all of America's client states. The scene in Thailand, for example, was described chillingly in the January, 29, 1972, *Far Eastern Economic Review:*

> In Udorn, the most striking thing is the town's apparent removal from the Indochina war. War's work here is as complex and sealed as in an American think-tank. And leisure is that of a computer-programmed technological society. Shortly after sunset, around a neon-lighted heart-shaped swimming pool in the garden of one of this city's many new hotels, East begins its nightly courtship of West. While officers and men of the US Air Force lounge in sports clothes, drinking Coca-Cola and Thai beer, Thai prostitutes of both sexes circle the pool, hand in hand. A jukebox drums out the insect noises of the tropical night with surfing music. A spotlighted white plaster female stands symbolically nude in the center of the fountain. By 9 P.M. the circling has stopped. Couples or groups take their leave for the night's activities. And overhead—almost drowned by the music, the buzz of air-conditioners, the propositions of rickshaw boys and the giggles of teen-aged girls on the arms of their American clients—US warplanes fly off into the night.

The Truth Most Hidden: America Is Fighting Whole Peoples, Whole Nations, Revolutions Which Already Have Happened

If it is difficult to summarize all these American strategies, it is because of their staggering arrogance. Americans simply assume they know what is best for the Vietnamese; Huntington, for example, calls his Western parliamentary system "a *natural* next step in *Vietnamese* development," as if it was indigenous to Asia and he a Vietnamese himself. Clearly the US war on Vietnam (and in all Indochina) is not only a matter of military force, but a *total assault on a people, a culture, a nation.*

American planners may still believe in their ultimate triumph, but that is only evidence of their *hubris,* the ancient Greek curse for those whose fatal error is in stretching too far in pursuit of power. In Vietnam, the US is attacking a people with a powerful identity and culture going back for centuries. Many other people have long since been absorbed into larger nation states, but the Vietnamese are exceptional in the degree to which their national identity has been formed in successful resistance to outside aggression and imperialism for thousands of years.

The Vietnamese myth of creation itself glorifies resistance. In this myth a woman gives birth to a strange little boy, who is called Holy Giong, and who is silent for three years, until one day messengers come asking for volunteers to resist the country's enemy. Holy Giong's first words are, "I will fight the enemy," and so he goes forth.

Victims of racism and great power chauvinism for thousands of years, the Vietnamese find nothing essentially new in the arrogance of the Americans. Today they are called "slopes," "dinks," "gooks," no differently than 2,000 years ago when the Chinese feudalists called their colony Giao Chi, meaning "big toes pointed at each other," a sneering insult to Vietnamese peasants.

A deep tradition of communalism has existed in Vietnamese villages for generations. People live in the presence of their ancestors' graves, working their traditional lands, sharing their experience and making decisions in common with full knowledge of each other's ways. A Vietnamese saying, that the "laws of the king are less powerful than the laws of the village," testifies to this decentralized and consensus-oriented way. It was a whole life in which one lived in company with "the living dead" (especially memorialized were those ancestors who lived and died for the nation; they are venerated as *everyone's* ancestors) and in harmony with the land. Natural calamities were as much a part of the recurrent cycle as foreign invasions, and the karma of the Vietnamese was shaped by these two forces more than any other.

The national literature of the Vietnamese, little of which has been translated into English, identifies the basis of their culture. Their most famous poet, Nguyen Du, wrote passages in the eighteenth century that fit the Americans exactly:

> *There were those who pursued power and glory*
> *Who dreamt of conquest and power.*
> *Why evoke the days of epic battles*
> *When subsequent misfortunes brought great sorrow?*
> *Their golden palaces crumbled*
> *And they envied a humble man's lot.*
> *Power and riches make many enemies . . .*

> *There were those who lived in curtained palaces,*
> *Priding themselves on their wealth and beauty.*
> *Then the storm came and thrones changed hands,*
> *No shelter could they find for their frail bodies.*
> *As the stream winds by the great palace,*
> *Nothing in this world remains still.*
> *Broken are the hairpins and the flower vases,*
> *Gone the animated voices and the laughter . . .*

> *There were those who wielded great power*
> *Whose red-ink characters decided men's fates,*
> *Who were fountains of knowledge and experience.*
> *But prosperity and power engender hatred . . .*

> *There were those who pursued riches*
> *Who lost appetite and sleep,*

With no children or relations to inherit their fortunes,
With no one to hear their last words.
Riches dissipate like passing clouds.
Living, they had their hands full of gold.
Departing from this world, they could take no single coin . . .

There were those at the head of proud armies
Who sacked palaces and overturned thrones.
In a display of might like storm and thunder,
Thousands were killed for the glory of one man.
Then came defeat and the battlefield was strewn with corpses.
The unclaimed bones are lying somewhere in a far-away land,
The rain is lashing down and the wind howling,
Who now will evoke their memory?

If this is the fate of their enemies, the fate of the Vietnamese is to endure suffering and be redeemed through it. This is the theme of Nguyen Du's eighteenth-century epic poem, *Kieu,* which is written about a young woman separated from her lover, who experiences constant degradation, betrayal, and attempts on her life until she meets him once again. Kieu's search, of course, is the search of the Vietnamese for unification. Her willingness to sacrifice everything for principle is set down in these famous lines:

It is better that I should sacrifice myself alone.
It matters little if a flower falls if the tree can keep its leaves
   green.

The effect of this culture on ordinary people has been described by the German author Peter Weiss in discussing with North Vietnamese the ideas of peasants who were just learning to read and write in the late sixties. Not well acquainted with foreign words, "they thought when they heard the word 'individualist' that it meant 'cannibal' . . ." One Vietnamese explained that "they had shared work together, lived together, and since time immemorial had made common cause against natural catastrophe and enemy attack."

The Americans have tried to destroy this cultural foundation while communists and other nationalists in Vietnam have tried to build on it. The US, through Diem, abolished village councils completely in the fifties, and only reopened the facade of village government in the late sixties. American bombing and ground missions destroy the ancestral graves and move people from their traditional farms and homes. The US policy has always favored the Catholic minority against the Buddhist majority, on the grounds that the Catholics were the most anti-communist: which is only a way of saying the Catholics were the most colonized by the French. Above all, the American concepts of individualism, success orientation, and materialism are foreign to the culture of Vietnam.

Communism in Vietnam grows from this cultural and national stem, however. The most serious modern difficulties of the Vietnamese Communist Party, for example, seem to have occurred when "foreign models" of socialism have been attempted, as in the fifties when Chinese-style, large-scale collective agriculture was attempted, met with resistance, and was modified. The officials of North Vietnam, and of the People's Revolutionary Government (PRG) in South Vietnam, many of them poets and intellectuals like Ho Chi Minh, lay claim legitimately to the long, proud tradition of national resistance to the Chinese, French, British, Japanese, and Americans.

The Vietnamese communist attitude toward Nguyen Du and the poem *Kieu* gives an example of the "natural" basis of communism in Vietnamese society (as opposed to the kind of "natural" Western institutions Huntington would introduce). This epic poem, written in the period of feudalism, contains many doctrines which could be considered contrary to progressive thought in general, or to a Communist Party trying to develop its country and fight a major war. There is a sense of

resignation and fatalism in Nguyen Du's Buddhism, as w
he cries out in one poem about the oppressed:

Such was their destiny, no one knows the reason.

Life in this world is like a bubble,
Buddha said: "All is but vanity."
Follow His guidance and be freed from the endless
Cycle of Existences . . .

His Mercy brings salvation to all.
No anxiety about being or not being.

Nguyen Du himself was hardly radical; he was a mandarin whose distress at the corruption of the feudal regime was not as great as his hostility toward the popular masses. He opposed the Tayson rebellion of 1789, the most famous of Vietnam's peasant movements. Under French colonialism, which gained its first foothold in Vietnam with the defeat of the Taysons and the return of the corrupt Nguyen dynasty in 1802, the poem *Kieu* was deliberately used to promote a passive and tragic sense in the Vietnamese people. The French were to be another in Kieu's (Vietnam's) succession of "patrons"; this was her permanent karma.

Thus Vietnamese revolutionary nationalists had every reason to fight against the propagation of the Kieu myth as part of a tradition keeping the Vietnamese in bondage (Buddhism) and further exploited by the French. Indeed, many revolutionaries denounced the poem for "weakening the ideals" of the nation and for substituting neurotic fatalism for a revolutionary will. But the communist intellectuals took a nationalist position which at once attacked the cultural co-optation of the French and the anti-nationalist radicalism of other "left" parties. They condemned as "nationalism without political content" the doctrines of the Westernized Vietnamese intellectuals who proclaimed *Kieu* as the "entire soul" and experience of the Vietnamese. But they also opposed the interpretation of *Kieu* as being a poem limited by feudal consciousness. Instead, they celebrate *Kieu* as a timeless documentary which "finds an echo in the hearts of all victims of wickedness" and which encourages "sincerity of sentiment and uprightness of character." They view the feudal era limits on Nguyen Du as inevitable, since there was no visible alternative to the social order he experienced. They deny it will have a "dissolving influence" on popular spirit because of its fatalism, for in real history the Vietnamese "have always managed to lift up their heads and fight again after the worst catastrophes." *Kieu* today remains as treasured as ever in communist Vietnam, even under a government which practices a "scientific socialism" supposedly contrary to Buddhist precepts of karma. One North Vietnamese official describes what has happened this way: "From Buddhism we have learned charity; the revolution has provided an instrument for making charity possible in this world."

The concept of popular revolutionary warfare using guerrilla tactics and strategy also has deep roots in Vietnamese history. Throughout the centuries the Vietnamese have been invaded and overrun by large forces with superior weapons, forcing reliance on the masses for national defense. The origins of guerrilla warfare go back to the thirteenth century when Kublai Khan invaded with 500,000 troops (Vietnamese today proudly draw a parallel between Kublai Khan's numbers and those at the high point of American intervention). In the thirteenth century occupation a debate arose among Vietnamese officials about whether or not to fight and if so, how to do it. The matter was settled in favor of fighting by a huge gathering of thousands of village elders whom the Vietnamese leadership consulted. This was the beginning of the concept of the people's war. Small units were formed and the local peasant population was armed. After several years of warfare by harassment, the Vietnamese triumphed in 1288 by penetrating the Mongol rear base and sinking ships full of reinforcements in the Bach Dang River.

Guerrilla warfare was also employed during the reign of Le Loi in the fifteenth century against the Ming Dynasty. The master Vietnamese military strategist then was Nguyen Trai who fought for ten years, built liberated zones, concentrated his attacks on enemy supply lines, and stressed propagandizing among the enemy troops. Nguyen Trai's military philosophy was expressed in these verses:

> *Those in authority are the ship*
> *But the people are the sea*
> *The sea carries the ship*
> *And causes it to capsize.*

> *The army should have only one goal*
> *To defeat the enemy*
> *The commander should have only one task*
> *To serve the people.*

Massive peasant revolts have occurred throughout Vietnamese history, the most famous being the Tayson revolt between 1770 and 1790. The leadership under Nguyen Hue climaxed its success with surprise attacks during Tet in 1789. Two hundred years later, during 1968, South Vietnamese students openly celebrated Nguyen's Hue's 1789 feat with dramatic celebrations in the streets of Saigon just prior to the NLF offensive. American officials were completely blind to the parallel being enacted before their eyes. General Westmoreland was even presented with a statuette of Nguyen Hue by a Vietnamese "friend" a few weeks before Tet 1968.

The Vietnamese have long understood that political difficulties will arise in the homeland of their enemies during a protracted and frustrating war. One Chinese emperor in the feudal ages had this to say about his Vietnamese enemies:

Why should we take Chinese troops, forces, money, and supplies and waste them in such a hot, desolate, and useless place? It is definitely in the class of not being worth it. . . . Even if we chase a Nguyen Hue how can we guarantee there will not be more Nguyen Hues coming out to cause trouble? The environment of that place is not hospitable.

American strategists today recognize the deep historical roots of people's war, but incorrectly believe that the ARVN can be turned into a People's Army. One such planner is Brian Jenkins of RAND who has written a "for official use only" working paper for the Pentagon entitled "A People's Army for South Vietnam." Written in September, 1971, Jenkins' paper recognizes that the ARVN are overdependent on French and American military concepts, particularly in their reliance on artillery and air power. Jenkins further recognizes that the NLF has the only organization which can properly be called a People's Army. He urges that the ARVN become a People's Army, noting that "the concept is deeply rooted in Vietnamese history and military traditions." In the style of other American planners, Jenkins proposes that the fundamental change be introduced covertly and by elite means: ". . . we must not make it look like another foreign import. A more correct tack would be to insinuate the idea with a few key individuals at the top including Thieu and Khiem and some of the more favorably disposed senior officers, and then quietly support them."

What planners like Jenkins fail to realize is that a People's Army can only be created against a foreign occupying force, never in the service of such a force. People's war depends ultimately on arousing the consciousness of the majority of the people, not on insinuating new ideas through their elite.

Vietnamese concepts of human nature as interpreted by Vietnamese Marxism-Leninism are a natural and consistent development from Vietnamese tradition—especially Confucian tradition. According to both of these doctrines, the vast majority of people are essentially good, and if racist or aggressive traits show up in them, they are caused by institutions and a lack of information and experience. This doctrine was expressed in a Vietnamese textbook *Nho Giao* (Confucianism) by Tran Trong Kim written during the 1920s and read by a generation of intellectuals which included Ho Chi Minh. Tran Trong Kim was hardly a nationalist himself; in fact, he was prime minister under the Japanese occupation. But his teachings are little different than those accepted by Vietnamese communists today:

> The overwhelming majority of people, who are called middle or average people become good or bad according to the education and the customs they acquire. These average people, all of them, can be educated. This applies to every sort of person, in every position in society from every race and country. Everyone can be educated to be good. The aim of Confucianism is to educate people so they become human and devoted.

Echoes of the Confucian text are found in the 1942–43 prison diary of Ho Chi Minh. One poem called "Midnight" describes the prisoners in his cell, and by implication, all of humanity:

> *Faces all have an honest look in sleep.*
> *Only when they wake does good*
> *or evil show in them.*
> *Good and evil are not qualities born in man:*
> *More often than not, they arise*
> *from our education.*

In general, it can be said that the cooperative values of Vietnamese communism are far more harmonious and indigenous than the values of competitive capitalism. Public ownership and planning, for example, are consistent with traditional concepts of property and historic demands of the peasantry; private ownership and personal exploitation are associated with feudalism, colonialism, and foreign occupation. Village democracy and consensus forms of decision-making have been preserved under socialism alongside voting, but the parliamentary "representative" system, with its competition and personality cults, is associated with France, the United States, and the failed promise of the Geneva Conference. Local control, creative improvisation and initiative, and self-reliance are age-old tendencies which, if anything, have been accelerated because of the needs for decentralization and province-level autonomy in people's war; these are antithetical to corporate and bureaucratic control. Moreover, even where new policies and institutions have been created in socialist Vietnam, considerable care is usually taken to blend the wisdom of tradition with the discoveries of science. In agriculture, for instance, one North Vietnamese study speaks of "technical–scientific committees" in the cooperatives, "comprising experienced old peasants working together with young people" from the technical colleges; these committees work together on "experimental plots where they try out new techniques." In public health, also, there is an emphasis on preserving and enriching the knowledge of herbs and other traditional medical practice alongside the introduction of scientific knowledge gained from the "advanced" countries.

If the cultural basis of Vietnamese communism lies in Vietnamese history, the class base lies in the more specific history of French colonialism, which forced Vietnam out of its feudal/mandarin system into a colonial one with an impoverished working class in the coal mines and rubber plantations. French domination drove many of the mandarin class, and especially the patriotic scholars and intellectuals, into nationalist resistance. The only realistic path to national independence under those conditions was through an organized movement, spurred by the radical nationalists but composed mainly of the great majority of the people who were peasants and workers. No really significant "national capitalist class" was allowed to develop under the French who kept even the "educated" and Catholicized Vietnamese in completely subservient status. Out of this combination of circumstances, and in the wake of the Japanese-Russian war of 1905, World War I, and the Russian Revolution, an Indochinese Communist Party was formed under the leadership of Ho Chi Minh and many of the ministers still heading the DRV (North Vietnamese Government) today. This party became the inheritor of the nationalist tradition. It was the only well-organized vehicle of the nationalist movement from the 1930s forward. It has proved in practice to be the most accurate prophet of what Vietnam's enemies would attempt next; the most effective defender of Vietnam's traditions; the successful instrument of national independence; the organization which has made improvements on the critical problems of land reform and agricultural production; literacy and general education; public health; and the only vehicle which has effectively united a majority of the people for self-defense against heavily equipped foreign invaders.

This does not mean that North Vietnam or the NLF are perfect, are correct about world politics, are a "model" for other countries, or anything else which this analysis might seem to imply. Americans unfortunately fall into too many absolute categories of judgment about revolutionary movements and socialist countries, instead of feeling a solidarity with the *process* of struggles against colonialism and underdevelopment, while still assuming the natural existence of plentiful problems. My own view of the Vietnamese revolutionaries happens to be that they are extraordinary, a fact which American ethnocentrism sadly erases. But it is not necessary to share that judgment in order to agree that *objectively* the Vietnamese have gone through historical struggles and created institutions that qualify them completely as a legitimate and dignified nation, no matter how much they are dismissed as a "fourth-rate power" by Western diplomacy and propaganda.

Perhaps the most important fact about Vietnam, which is virtually kept a secret from the American public, is that the Vietnamese carried out a successful national revolution under communist leadership, and established a new government in 1945–46 *from one end of the country to the other*. They created a flag, armed forces, postal service, and other communications machinery, held nationwide elections, set up administrative offices, collected taxes and issued currency, and began emergency programs to combat famine and illiteracy. It was against this reality that the French, with US support, intervened for the nine-year war that ended at Dien Bien Phu. What America has been fighting in Vietnam is not "aggression from the North" nor a "civil war," as the doves like to insist, but a *successful revolutionary nation, as valid in its claim to self-determination as any in history.*

What is happening in Vietnam is exactly the opposite of conventional Western doctrine, which portrays communist revolution as a process of destroying the present for the sake of an abstract future. Instead of warding off this "communist takeover" or "aggression," the United States is facing a united people who are fighting to protect gains which they had already made. The communist movement in Vietnam fights on the basis of the August, 1945, Revolution which created the Democratic Republic of Vietnam—the land reform, education, and public health programs inaugurated then; the military victory of Dien Bien Phu in 1954; the Geneva agreements guaranteeing reunification by 1956; the industrial progress achieved in the North in the fifties, and so on. These are people fighting not simply *against* their oppressors but also *for* policies and institutions which they were beginning to build when the Americans intervened, and which they have gone on trying to develop.

This is where America's *hubris* begins, in stubbornly refusing for twenty-five years to accept this reality, in thinking that reality can be manipulated, bombed, and terrorized into nothingness and finally replaced with a "reality" created entirely in the United States.

It is this hidden side of the Vietnam war which is most difficult for Americans to accept. The terms of controversy about Vietnam usually have been ethnocentric: hawks versus doves debating the US interest, the cost, the morality for Americans, the legality, and so forth. Those who identify too closely with the NLF or North Vietnam are dismissed as "propagandists," as if the only "objective" view would find serious fault with all sides in the war. As a result we are insulated from the horrors which those "other" Vietnamese, hidden in the liberated zones and behind the DMZ, have actually had to endure. We also are left in confusion about how any people could survive all the military, economic, and diplomatic pressures of the US for so many years. The only explanations given tend to be stereotypes about Vietnamese "stoicism" or willingness to sacrifice individual life for their cause. The Orient remains inscrutable. We Americans, with all our television and communications, become the most isolated people in the world, not because we lack the technical means of communication but because we are not allowed to see outside of the national and cultural framework dominating us.

In part this is a deliberate process. The Pentagon Papers finally show that US planners have *known all along* that the Vietnamese had made an effective and popular revolution. The US intervened anyway, and decided as a necessary corollary that the truth would have to be kept from the American people.

Occasional public statements and documents from the Pentagon Papers contain ample evidence of this:

> . . . General Big Minh's opinion expressed very privately yesterday that the Viet Cong are steadily gaining in strength; have more of the population on their side than has the GVN; that arrests are continuing and the prisons are full; that there is great graft and corruption in the Vietnamese administration of our aid; and that the "heart of the Army is not in the war." All this by Vietnamese No. 1 General is now echoed by Secretary of Defense Thuan (see my 542) who wants to leave country. (*Henry Cabot Lodge, cable to Kennedy "for President only" September 19, 1963*)

Nevertheless the US under Kennedy helped organize the fateful coup and killing of Diem a few weeks later. After Kennedy was assassinated, the new US President received a similar assessment from McNamara:

> Viet Cong progress has been great during the period since the coup, with my best guess being that the situation has in fact been deteriorating in the countryside since July to a far greater extent than we realized because of our undue dependence on distorted Vietnamese reporting. The Viet Cong now control very high proportions of the people in certain key provinces . . . particularly those directly south and west of Saigon [the Delta, where most of the South Vietnamese live]. The Strategic Hamlet Program was seriously overextended in those provinces. . . . In these key provinces, the Viet Cong have destroyed almost all major roads, and are collecting taxes at will. (*Memorandum to Johnson, December 21, 1963*)

At the time of the 1964 US election, another turning point, the appraisal by Ambassador Maxwell Taylor was consistent with the year before. He wrote privately on November 27, 1964, of the "continuing weakness of the Saigon government," the "war weariness and hopelessness" in the cities, a "factionalism" and lack of "national spirit," and a collapse of counter-insurgency so total that only "heroic treatment [could] assure survival." However, he wrote with awe and respect of the other side, which seemed to be having no such problems:

> The ability of the Viet Cong continuously to rebuild their units and to make good their losses is one of the mysteries of this guerrilla war. . . . Not only do Viet Cong units have the recuperative powers of the phoenix, but they have an *amazing ability to maintain morale.* Only in rare cases have we found evidences of bad morale among Viet Cong prisoners or recorded in captured Viet Cong documents.

Although in the October, 1964, *Foreign Affairs,* CIA General Edward Lansdale warned that "the Communists have let loose a revolutionary idea in Vietnam and . . . it will not die by being ignored, bombed or smothered by us," that is precisely what was proved with the commencement of Operation Rolling Thunder in February, 1965. In September, 1965, the American public was given this frank revelation by James Reston:

> Even Premier Ky told this reporter today that the Communists were closer to the people's yearnings for social justice and an independent life than his own government. (*The New York Times, September 1, 1965*)

Nevertheless, American planners cynically hoped that the level of popular support for the enemy would wither under each "turn of the screw," and indeed this speculation was fueled by the usual pseudo-scientific RAND reports purporting to show "VC spirit flagging." But as early as January, 1966, McNamara's assistant McNaughton was aware that the bombing was a failure. In a January 19 memo he acknowledged once again that "the GVN political infrastructure is moribund; weaker than the VC infrastructure among most of the rural population."

One month later, on February 27, Henry Cabot Lodge
acknowledged publicly that

> For years now in Southeast Asia, the only people who have
> been doing anything for the little man—to lift him up—have
> been the Communists.

This was no late discovery, as some who cling to the
"mistake" theory of the Vietnam war might claim. This understanding by US policy-makers that they were intervening
against a popular revolutionary force goes back to the very
origins of the decision to replace the French after Geneva.
At that time, a decided and continual hawk, Joseph Alsop,
made a fascinating journey deep into Vietminh zones in the
Mekong Delta, the southernmost part of Vietnam, to see for
himself the Ho Chi Minh-led revolutionaries. He later wrote
an article for the *New Yorker* on June 25, 1955, which must
have shocked official Washington. Alsop wrote:

> I would like to be able to report—I had hoped to be able to
> report—that on that long, slow canal trip to Vinh Binh
> [Mekong Delta], I saw all the signs of misery and oppression
> that have made my visits to East Germany like nightmare
> journeys into 1984. But it was not so. . . . At first it was
> difficult to conceive of a Communist government's genuinely
> "serving the people." I could hardly imagine a Communist
> government that was also a popular goverment and almost a
> democratic government. But this is just the sort of govern-
> ment the palm-hut state actually was while the struggle with
> the French continued. The Vietminh could not possibly have
> carried on the resistance for one year, let alone nine years,
> without the people's strong united support.

With the publication of the Pentagon Papers we can
now discover how embarrassing the Alsop article was, how
the CIA was working to involve the US in a Vietnam commitment, and how at that time the journalism establishment

was being counted on as propagandists. All this is revealed by the 1954–55 report of the secret Saigon Military Mission (SMM), an American team of spies and saboteurs headed by "the Ugly American" himself, Edward G. Lansdale. The same journalism establishment which was willing to publish the Pentagon Papers in 1971 could have done it fifteen years before, were they not themselves collaborating then with the CIA. General Lansdale wrote of getting together privately with the top American journalists in Asia:

> Till and Peg Durdin of the *N.Y. Times,* Hank Lieberman of the *N.Y. Times,* Homer Bigart of the *N.Y. Herald Tribune,* John Mecklin of *Life-Time,* and John Roderick of Associated Press have been *warm friends of SMM* and *worked hard to penetrate the fabric of French propaganda and give the US an objective account* of events in Vietnam. The group met with us at times to analyze objectives and motives of *propaganda* known to them, *meeting at their own request as US citizens. These mature and responsible news correspondents performed a valuable service for their country.*

Lansdale's mission, among its many foolish and ugly tricks, was busy putting out phony messages from a fabricated "Vietminh Resistance Committee" to Vietminh cadre who were being regrouped temporarily to the North in accord with the Geneva settlement. These false leaflets were supposed to be spread through the Mekong Delta, where Joseph Alsop was traveling. The leaflets were designed to scare the Vietminh regroupees by saying they would be kept below the decks of ships safe "from imperialist air and submarine attacks" on the way North, and also requested they bring warm clothing. According to Lansdale's memo, "the warm clothing item would be coupled with a verbal rumor campaign that Vietminh were being sent into China as railroad laborers." The effect was to create confusion and fear of "deportation" to the communist North.

Lansdale deliberately planned to have this rumor reach Alsop, who then could be expected to report a grim story of "communist deportation" and "forced labor" to the American people, presumably just the sort of story Alsop "had hoped to report" but couldn't find. Instead Lansdale failed:

> Distribution in Camau was made while columnist Alsop was on his visit there which led to his sensational, *gloomy* articles later; *our soldier "Vietminh" failed in an attempt to get the leaflet into Alsop's hands in Camau;* Alsop was never told this story. . . .

What was "gloomy" about Alsop's articles? That they praised the Vietminh administration, that they revealed the communist government extended all the way to the southernmost tip of Vietnam? This could be "gloomy" only to Americans who were planning to supplant that administration with that of Diem, and who desperately needed the American press to print convincing propaganda to sell the American people on the Vietnam venture.

This nauseating deceit has characterized American policy ever since. Its effects have been felt most heavily by the Vietnamese people, as the bombs and shells rain down on the social structure they have so painfully built. But the effects on the American people are awful as well. Hundreds of thousands of American GIs have been killed or wounded for a lie. More than $100 billion in tax money has been spent to finance a lie. And in the process of being lied to, the American people have been filled with confusion and surrounded by a secretive decision-making structure they know nothing about.

The only people who have really known these secrets have been the small circle of government officials and their various advisers who have pursued the Vietnam policy for all these years. These individuals are shielded from public scrutiny because of "national security," and their power is constantly being further centralized, reaching an apex under

Nixon and Kissinger. So autocratic is this structure that, according to the Pentagon Papers, basic Vietnam decisions were made in consultation with a group picked by Johnson and called the "Wise Men."

The Wise Men, otherwise called the Senior Informal Advisory Group, were described by *The New York Times* as men who had served in "high government posts or had been presidential advisers during the last twenty years." These men, who apparently gave the "decisive advice" about changing the war strategy in 1968 after having generally been severe war hawks until that time, represent the private centers of power in America:

Dean Acheson, Secretary of State under Truman;

George Ball, Undersecretary of State under Kennedy and Johnson;

General Omar Bradley, former Chairman of the Joint Chiefs of Staff;

McGeorge Bundy, "special assistant for national security" under Kennedy and Johnson, now president of the Ford Foundation;

Arthur Dean, like nearly all the others a corporate lawyer, also US negotiations head in Korea;

Douglas Dillon, banker, Undersecretary of State under Eisenhower, Secretary of the Treasury under Kennedy and Johnson;

Abe Fortas, Supreme Court Justice and a prime lawyer for big business;

Arthur Goldberg, Ambassador to the UN;

Henry Cabot Lodge, twice Ambassador to South Vietnam, former Ambassador to the UN, Nixon's vice-presidential candidate in 1960;

John J. McCloy, one of the most powerful corporate lawyers shuttling in and out of government, Roosevelt's Secretary of War, Truman's High Commissioner for Germany, president

of the World Bank, chairman of the board of Chase Man-
hattan Bank;

Robert Murphy, ranking diplomat from the beginning of the
Cold War;

General Matthew Ridgway, US Commander in Korea, Army
Chief of Staff, member of the Board of Directors of Colt Industries;

Cyrus Vance, Deputy Secretary of Defense, one of the top US
negotiators in Cyprus, Korea, Vietnam.

These Wise Men advocated what has become the Nixon
program. Johnson was described as "deeply shaken" by their
decision, and soon retired from office. So much for American
democracy; it seems to work already in America the way
Huntington proposes it should work in Saigon. Malcolm X
said it: the chickens will come home to roost.

Why Vietnam? Ask, Why America?

American expansion, both economic and geographic, was not
accomplished without a judicious application of force.
(*Henry Kissinger,* Nuclear Weapons and Foreign Policy)

That the cover of lies is only now beginning to be stripped
from the reality of Vietnam by sources like the Pentagon
Papers should of course be a cause for outrage. But more than
that, it should raise the question of what other secrets have
been hidden or conveniently buried from the American people
about our whole history? The real lesson of Vietnam is what
it may yet teach us about our genocidal history, about the
real identity of American civilization as understood by its
victims.

The war which is climaxing on the Asian mainland actually began a long time ago in the United States. The origins of the war lie in the origins of America. In fact, we might see the war as the latest phase of a 500-year war between Western settlers—the English, French, and Spanish especially—and the native inhabitants of lands which the settlers have sought to conquer. That deluded and murderous adventurer Christopher Columbus, after all, was searching for the fabled Far East and thought he found it here in the Western Hemisphere. That is why he mistakenly called the native people "Indians."

Columbus, taking possession of what he named San Salvador on October 12, 1492, described the natives as generous people who "loved their neighbors as themselves" and "who took all and gave all, such as they had, with good will." As a typical imperialist, Columbus was confused by this attitude of sharing, which made him conclude "they were a people very deficient in everything." But they "should be good servants" and Columbus believed they would "easily be made Christians, for it appeared to me they had no creed." Columbus apparently kidnapped six natives to bring back to his Highnesses "that they may learn to talk." When the natives resisted the Spanish gold-seekers who burned their villages, hundreds of thousands of them were killed—nearly the whole island population being exterminated only a decade after Columbus' arrival.

Amerigo Vespucci, for whom our country is named, encountered similar cultures a few years later. He found the natives "barbarous" because they ate not at fixed times "but as often as they please," and "shameless" because they urinated in front of others, but at least "they showed themselves desirous of copulating with us Christians." He found them living in a sensual "epicurean" way; collectively, often in houses with hundreds of residents; and in a communal economy:

. . . they neither buy nor sell. In short, they live and are *contented with what nature gives them.* The wealth which we affect in this our Europe and elsewhere, such as *gold, jewels, pearls and other riches, they hold of no value at all.* . . .

As it was in the beginning, it is now. When Hubert Humphrey spoke of "spreading the Great Society to Asia" in 1968 while millions of Asians "who were content with few things" were being ruined and displaced, it was no different in essence from those who came here to create a New World long ago and in the process deceived, manipulated, killed, and subjugated the tribal communities. Our most (supposedly) "progressive" leaders ever since have combined their idealism with genocide. Few Americans realize, for instance, that their President Abraham Lincoln fought and even reenlisted in the Black Hawk War in Illinois. There are countless other examples, but the point here is not to explore American history in depth; the point is simply to note the parallels between the Indian Wars and the Indochina war, and these are amazingly close.

The native Americans and the people of Indochina may share not only a common enemy but also common origins. Anthropologists appear certain that the peoples of the American Southwest, at least, came over the Bering Strait from the lower parts of Asia.

These people lived in a total culture, in harmony with the natural world, close to their ancestors, typically considering the earth their mother and the sun their father. The land and waters belonged to everyone. This attitude was counterposed absolutely to that of the settlers who believed in the principles of man against nature, in private property, and in competition in relationships between people.

The native cultural attitudes, and the threat to them which the settlers represented, were spoken of by Sitting Bull in 1877:

[*100*]

Behold my brothers, the Spring has come; the earth has received the embraces of the sun and we shall soon see the results of that love!

Every seed is awakened and so has all animal life. It is through this mysterious power that we too have our being, and we therefore yield to our neighbors, even our animal neighbors, the same right as ourselves, to inhabit this land.

Yet, hear me, people, we have now to deal with another race—small and feeble when our fathers first met them but now great and overbearing. Strangely enough they have a mind to till the soil and *the love of possession is a disease with them.* These people have made many rules that the rich may break but the poor may not. They take their tithes from the poor and weak to support the rich and those who rule.

They claim this Mother of ours, the earth, for their own and fence their neighbors away; they deface her with their buildings and their refuse. That nation is like a spring freshet that overruns its banks and destroys all who are in its path.

We cannot dwell side by side. Only seven years ago we made a treaty by which we were assured that the buffalo country should be left to us forever. Now they threaten to take that away from us. My brothers, shall we submit or shall we say to them: "First kill me before you take possession of my Fatherland. . . ."

"Great and overbearing" missionaries were among the first to arrive on this continent as the French priests did in Indochina on what they commonly called their "civilizing" missions. Behind them were the gunboats and cannon representing a new and overwhelming power; in both cases, some (definitely a minority) of the native people were won away from traditional rites to the new life-style of Christianity. This meant, in practice, becoming traitors to their people, serving the interests of the invaders, becoming the client or neo-colonial "elite." In Vietnam, those converted to the Catholic Church by the French became the base of anti-communism and the subadministrators for the French interests. We should not forget the considerable degree to which the American Catholic Church pressured the US to intervene in Vietnam as the French were being repelled. As the investigations by Robert Scheer several years ago indicate, the American "Vietnam Lobby" included the Catholic hierarchy and senators like John Kennedy. When Ngo Dinh Diem was groomed in the US to become future leader of South Vietnam, he stayed at Maryknoll seminaries in New Jersey and New York. His chief Catholic encouragers were Dr. Tom Dooley, who wrote passionately of "diseased, mutilated Asians fleeing from the godless cruelties of Communism," and Cardinal Spellman, who condemned the Geneva settlement as a sell-out "betraying the sacred trust of our forefathers" to a bunch of "Red rulers' godless goons."

Christianity and capitalism never were in conflict in transforming the land of the native Americans, nor have they been in Southeast Asia. Just like missionaries on the American frontier, Dr. Dooley had this to say about the disinterestedness of his relationship to all those savages he ministered to:

> Rest assured, we continually explained to thousands of refugees, as individuals and in groups, that *only in a country which permits companies to grow large could such fabulous charity be found. With every one of the thousands of capsules of terramycin and with every dose of vitamins on a baby's tongue, these words were said: Dai La My-Quoc Vietn-tro (This is American aid).*

The same thought was put more regally ninety years before by A. B. Riegnier, one of the leading theoreticians of France's role in Indochina:

> France can dream again of finding overseas not only the activity necessary to its commerce, for the development of its industry and the creation of outlets for the future, but it can

also begin again the noble civilizing mission that has always given it such a high place in the world.

The native Americans had a highly intricate structure of government (as even Benjamin Franklin, no friend of theirs, acknowledged with respect) and an economic system which initially saved the settlers (by showing them how to raise crops). Their culture was magnificent. The historical politics, agriculture, and culture of Indochina were equally developed, complex, and magnificent before colonialism. Yet in both cases the natives have been regarded as savages. John Smith called the Jamestown natives a "viporous brood"; today the Vietnamese are "gooks." The phrase "Viet Cong" was invented by American psychological warriors as a derogatory description meaning something like "Viet-commies." Similarly, the white settlers described their feared enemies as "Apache" and "Sioux," both terms originally meaning "enemy." General Sheridan who said "the only good Injun is a dead Injun" is echoed today by Ambassador Godley in Cambodia saying the "only good communist is six feet under ground." The massacres at My Lai in 1968 are part of a consistent tradition of sadistic atrocities inflicted by whites on their native enemies, recalling the infamous nineteenth-century slaughters at Sand Creek and Wounded Knee. In all these cases, peaceful villagers, unarmed, were murdered at point-blank range, with their ears and especially genitals seeming to be trophies and targets of the hysterical whites. The "body count" began in the Wild West, not in Vietnam, as one can observe in any Western film where the US soldiers kill hundreds of natives in any given battle.

The defeated natives, at least those who survived the wars, were placed in reservations essentially the same as the "strategic hamlets" of Southeast Asia. There, for "security," they were kept from their traditional lands, forced to live cramped together, and kept dependent on horribly inadequate food rations from the US government.

Forced marches and deportation were imposed on the native Americans as they are in Indochina today, with whole communities ordered to move from their sacred lands, then forcibly pushed at gunpoint on marches which cost innumerable lives. In the process, the cultural basis of life—the very relationship to the land—was eroded, and in every case the new lands were inadequate to meet the surviving natives' needs. Most tribes were moved again and again, until they were destroyed and the survivors made into helpless wards.

Classic counter-insurgency "resource denial" techniques were used constantly in the West, perhaps most infamously by Kit Carson against the Navahos. The rebellious tribe was given until July 20, 1863, to go to its assigned reservation. When they refused, Carson began a systematic military campaign of starving them rather than fighting directly. He ran off their sheep and horses, destroyed their corn and 2,000 peach trees, denying the Navahos even the tree bark, to force a surrender. The starving, freezing Navahos gave in at Canyon de Chelly, Colorado, in January, 1864. A similar approach has been used on hundreds of missions in Vietnam.

Not just "resource denial," however, but outright extermination of the buffalo took place. The beautiful Plains buffalo, which provided not only nourishment, clothing, shelter, and weapons but also a spiritual friend to the tribes, were utterly killed off, their numbers dropping from over 50 million to less than 800 in only twenty years, 1870–90. The *Washington Post* of December 28, 1971, quotes two American scientists saying that the

> massive defoliation, crop destruction bombing and plowing of Indochina can be viewed as a modern counterpart to the extermination of the bison in the American West . . . as destructive an influence on the social fabric of Indochinese life

as did the ecocide of the American West upon the American Indians.

As in Indochina, the settlers of America knew consciously what they were doing, including the injustice and brutality, yet justified it on the same grounds that American planners do today. The US Secretary of the Interior in 1851 described most Indian violence as springing from "dire necessity." The advancing white settlers forced them "to relinquish their fertile lands" and drove them to "sterile regions," where, "impelled by hunger, they seize the horses, mules and cattle of the pioneers." The pioneers then punished the Indians, and the Indians retaliated, and "a desolating war, attended with a vast sacrifice of blood and treasure, ensues."

There was hope for the Indian, however, just as there is today for the uprooted Vietnamese. As one agent stated the universal principle:

> With the buffalo gone, and their pony herds being constantly decimated by the inroads of horse thieves, *they must soon adopt, in all its varieties, the way of the white man.*

This "way" was the way of the market economy and its ethos, just as it is today in Asia. Here are the unvarnished words of the official report of the Interior Secretary for 1851:

> To tame a savage you must tie him down to the soil. You must make him understand the value of property, and the benefits of its separate ownership. You must appeal to those selfish principles implanted by Divine Providence in the nature of man for the wisest of purposes, and make them minister to civilization and refinement. You must encourage the appropriation of lands by individuals; attach them to their homes by the ties of interest; . . . and *they should be taught to look forward to the day when they may be elevated to the dignity of American citizenship. . . .*

By means like these we shall soon reap our reward in

the suppression of Indian depredations; in the diminution of the expenses of the Department of War; in a valuable addition to our productive population; in the increase of our agriculture and commerce; and in the proud consciousness that we have removed from our national escutcheon the stain left on it by our acknowledged injustice to the Indian race.

There was not exactly a "green revolution" on the frontier, but there was the equally "promising" Allotment Act of 1877. The purpose, according to one study, was "to make the Indians more like white landowning Americans by giving Indians with families 160 acres, and single ones 80 acres." As with "land reform" in Vietnam this plan assumed the "legality" of the original confiscation of the native's land, then generously reallocated the land to its first inhabitants in an utterly foreign property ownership framework. And again like Vietnam, this absurd "reform" failed even in its own objectives because of corruption. Sixty percent of the land supposedly designated for Indians ended up being owned by whites.

Having lost to the settlers their lands, the hunting grounds, their essential means of subsistence, the natives ultimately became dependent on the "Great White Father" for food, supplies, ammunition, farm equipment, entirely losing their self-reliance. In Vietnam the same process of making the natives dependent on Western technology through trade is underway on a grand scale.

Cultural destruction was the outcome. Forbidden to teach their language, attending white-controlled schools, living on reservations, disarmed, unemployed, the tribes gradually were disfigured into relics of themselves. The brothels of native prostitutes outside the stockades of the Wild West are paralleled today by the shanty-towns of prostitutes outside American bases in Vietnam; and drugs play the role in Asia that "firewater" did on the frontier.

All this was done, of course, with due regard for law

and the methods of negotiations. The United States government had a Gulf of Tonkin Resolution for every war it fought with the Indians: fully 200 major battles between 1600 and 1890. Nearly 400 treaties were negotiated, none of them honored by the US except those made with their clients (as in SEATO) by which more property and power were "legally" accumulated. As in Indochina today, the negotiating terms of the US always insisted on de facto submission of its opponents.

Native consciousness, in a final parallel, contained a sense that the people's karma would prevail over that of their oppressors. The epic poem *Kieu* condemns those who pursue power and glory, who live in curtained palaces, who head proud armies, and asks "who now will evoke their memory?" The famous 1855 speech of Chief Sealth forecasts the same haunting future for the oppressor:

> Tribe follows tribe, and nation follows nation, like the waves of the sea. It is the order of nature, and regret is useless. Your time of decay may be distant, but it will surely come, for even the white man . . . cannot be exempt from the common destiny. We may be brothers after all; we will see.
>
> And when the last red man shall have perished, and the memory of my tribe shall have become a myth among the white men, these shores will swarm with the invisible dead of my tribe, and when your children's children think themselves alone in the field, the store, the shop, upon the highway, or in the silence of the pathless woods, they will not be alone. . . .
>
> At night, when the streets of your cities and villages are silent and you think them deserted, they will throng with the returning hosts that once filled, and still love this beautiful land. The white man will never be alone.

It is common to hear doves describe Ho Chi Minh as the "George Washington of Vietnam," but it would be more accurate to call him a successful Tecumseh, one of the many great chiefs who tried to unite the many tribes into a common strategy of resistance. Ho's and Vietnam's success is attributable to different conditions from those which faced the native American. The natives were kept divided because of their hunting economy which required relatively small concentrations or pockets of people in each of the "hunting grounds"; this dispersal and shortage of resources made unity difficult. The Vietnamese, on the other hand, lived in tribal communities relatively dependent on each other in the delta of the Red River. Their unity was forged by economic interdependence, by coordination against natural catastrophe; their clans were never fully dissolved but evolved instead into the present-day system of villages. They were further united, in a way the native Americans were not, by tyrants and invaders, particularly the Chinese feudalists and the Vietnamese mandarins, who centralized Vietnam with an elaborate bureaucracy, but one which did not extend downward genocidally or disruptively into the tribal communes. The culture, art, and economy of the feudal era (promoting precious handicrafts, for example) developed a national culture although within a system of inequality. By contrast the Indians were never welded together "from above." When they were attacked, it was a direct and forcible challenge for the land they were living on. The economic and technical conditions to promote unity never existed sufficiently; their economic development was not for the glorification of their own native elite but became a degenerating pacification cycle of "self-help" services for their foreign conquerors. Moreover, being close to China and other Asian nations meant the Vietnamese were never as isolated as the Indians. The Asian continent was the scene of attempted colonizing but was never effectively settled by a new race of people. The Indians, however, were directly in the path of the dynamic opening phase of American capitalism's westward march; the American Revolution, in fact, was fought partly because Britain placed curbs on westward expansion. The Indochinese, on the other hand, while facing superior technology, are contending with a weaker imperialist policy and a more stagnant and overextended imperialist system. All these differences may explain the Vietnamese success, but cannot erase the parallels; it is almost as if the Indochinese are fighting as the incarnation of those "invisible dead" who fell on this continent in less favorable times.

The parallels are both consciously and subconsciously apparent in numerous ways in Indochina. The *Boston Globe* recently quoted a South Vietnamese nationalist, for instance, who pointed out to the US:

> You cannot defeat the other side militarily unless you devote the next 30 or 40 years to it. You can win if you keep killing for a generation. You simply exterminate all the Vietnamese—*the way you killed the Indians in America*—and there will be no more.

The vocabulary of the war reflects the Indian analogy, too. The US operates helicopters and gunships named Cheyenne, Mohawk, Chinook, Iroquois, Thunderchief. Bombing of the DRV was code-named "Rolling Thunder." NLF-controlled zones are called "Injun Country." A military manual is titled "Injun Fighting 1763—Counter-Insurgency 1963." Americans sitting armed in their helicopters are said to be "ridin' shotgun." ARVN troops in charge of village security are called Kit Carson Scouts. Honda-riding gangs of delinquents in Saigon are called "cowboys." Lyndon Johnson summarized it all in 1966 when he asked his Vietnam team, "Are those just words, or have you some coonskins on the wall?" (The war which began on the "New Frontier" now had its own Andrew Jackson.)

Strategic thinking shows similar influence, as three examples show:

(1) Maxwell Taylor, speaking on the problems of security around the strategic hamlets before the Fulbright Committee in 1966:

. . . I have often said it is very hard to plant the corn outside the stockade when the Indians are still around. We have to get the Indians farther away in many of the provinces to make good progress.

(2) Hugh Manke, head of the International Voluntary Service, testifying before the Kennedy subcommittee in 1971, on the relocation of 70,000 tribal people in the three-month period: by 1970, one half of 1,400 Montagnard villages were relocated at least once. Colonized Vietnamese, like the wife of Premier Ky, now are buying the old tribal lands for farming and lumbering. This, Manke testified, is "painfully reminiscent of the activities of American pioneers with regard to the Indian tribes." Manke spoke with a Captain Farrell, an adviser in Pleiku, who said "the Montagnards have to realize they are expendable," and who "compared the Montagnard problem to the Indian problem and said *we could solve the Montagnard problem like we solved the Indian problem.*"

(3) The GVN chief of Binh Dinh province, an NLF-controlled area, is Colonel Nguyen Van Chuc who, according to a February, 1972, *Los Angeles Times* headline, "Fights Reds with U.S. History." The colonel is urging people over television to adopt Dr. Frank Buchman's "Moral Re-Armament" principles. Trained as an engineer and soldier in the US, Chuc "has adopted many American mannerisms." One is using the "lessons of early American history to show the people why they should support the South Vietnamese government." The colonel says approvingly, not even aware of the cultural alteration which has occurred in himself, "*when Indians attacked a village, everyone got together and fired back.* . . . If the people in villages here gather together, they can defeat the Viet Cong." Those wanting a more graphic

lesson can see endless Western films in Saigon for ten cents each.

How to summarize this whole sickening indictment? We must first realize these analogies, grim as they are, only reveal a glimpse of our past. A fuller portrayal would include the process by which these new oppressors pillaged East African tribal communities to create the slave trade; how the Mexican people were fought, defeated, and annexed in the nineteenth century; how the oppressed peasant people in Ireland, Italy, and eastern Europe were driven by imperialism into the "modern" market system and finally became "Americans"; what happened similarly to the Puerto Ricans, Alaskans, Hawaiians, and the people of the Philippines, the Chinese who were "induced" here as laborers, the Japanese who were rounded up during World War II. The list of racist impositions stretches as far as the mind will inquire. We would understand finally the character structure of this Anglo-Protestant settler who is the model and standard of American society. We would see important questions in new historical ways. Is not Women's Liberation, for example, an historic challenge to the root cultural image of the American? Is not "integration"—as opposed to the universal harmony of the native American—a "subterfuge for white supremacy" as Stokely Carmichael insisted? Isn't the "revolutionary intercommunalism" of Huey Newton, which recognizes the positive value of separation as well as the necessity of ultimate harmony, a more meaningful concept than "integration"? We could also begin to ask ourselves, not the idle question of whether the Vietnam war is a "mistake," but the eighteenth-century question: was America a mistake? One history recalls that this was a burning question, and those who claimed the New World was a "mistake"

> charged that the discovery of America had led to the extermination of the native races, centuries of imperialist wars, the extension of slavery and the spread of deadly diseases.

Perhaps the most sweeping and still most dramatically condensed comment on what we face was made by the psychiatrist Carl Jung during a visit to the Taos Indians of New Mexico in the 1930s. I have taken a prose passage from Jung's autobiography and set in poetic form. An Indian said to Jung:

See how cruel the whites look.
Their lips are thin, their noses sharp, their faces furrowed
And distorted by folds.
Their eyes have a staring expression;
They are always seeking something.
What are they seeking?
The whites always want something; they are always uneasy
    and restless.
We do not know what they want.
We do not understand them.
We think they are mad.

When this Indian told Jung that the whites "think with their heads," the psychiatrist asked him what Indians think with. The Indian touched his heart, and inspired in Jung a vision:

This Indian had struck our vulnerable spot,
Unveiled a truth to which we are blind.
I felt rising within me like a shapeless mist
Something unknown yet deeply familiar.
And out of this mist, image upon image detached itself.

First, Roman legions smashing into the cities of Gaul,
And the keenly incised features of Julius Caesar, Scipio Africanus and Pompey.
I saw the Rcman eagle on the North Sea and on the banks of the White Nile.
Then I saw St. Augustine transmitting the Christian creed to the Britons on the tips of Roman lances,
And Charlemagne's most glorious forced conversions of the heathen.

*Then the pillaging and murdering bands of the Crusading
    Armies.
With a secret stab I realized the hollowness of that old ro-
    manticism about the Crusades.
Then followed Columbus, Cortez, and other conquistadores
    who
With fire, sword, torture and Christianity
Came down upon even these remote pueblos
Dreaming peacefully in the sun, their Father.
I saw, too, the peoples of the Pacific Islands
Decimated by firewater, syphilis and scarlet fever
Carried in the clothes the missionaries forced on them.*

*It was enough. What we from our point of view call coloni-
    zation,
Missions to the heathen, spread of civilization, etc.
Has another face—
The face of a bird of prey seeking with cruel intentness
For distant quarry—
A face worthy of a race of pirates and highwaymen.
All the eagles and other predatory creatures
That adorn our coats of arms seem to me
Apt psychological representatives of
Our true nature.*

Not only conservatives but many who consider themselves Marxists will object to Jung's insight as being too ex-
treme, condemning whites to permanent racism at worst, perhaps hopeless shame at best. But our victims experience us,
certainly, as a culture—as "Americans"—if not a race, and
it is crucial to know how we are defined by those America
oppresses. It will also be said that Americans are not alone
in committing genocide, and a familiar list of other tyrants
and murderers will be brought out in proof. Agreed; but
Jung's point does not exclude the possibility of other genocidal
civilizations, and in any case, in the specific epoch which is

ours, it is *Western* imperialism which has dominated the world.

One part of me wants to make distinctions that narrow the indictment, not only to defensively escape its sweep, but also to allow for understanding of certain positive elements in US history, and especially to permit hope for change rather than fatalism. Another part of me, which emerges when I see that our streets are silent while bombs fall on Indochina, wants to recognize a sense in which we all are responsible for degrees of complacency in the face of murder.

It is not adopting a monolithic fatalistic theory to think in terms of a total civilization—an economy, a politics, traditions, ideology—and the general impact on those it oppresses. Such an approach does not have to exclude the "good" in American history. But certainly it is time to rewrite the conventional comforting theories, shared by liberal and even some radical historians, that America's heritage is one of democratic ideals "marred" by capitalism and racism. It is valid to recall and renew the struggles of the American people for the rights to vote, to form trade unions, for civil rights, for an end to wars, as long as we also recall that these popular movements took place within a framework of neglect, racism, and often genocidal wars toward the oppressed outside white American structures.

We need no further evidence of the *potential* of the American people other than the fact, shown by the Pentagon Papers, that most decisions are made in secrecy. America's rulers have been the pirates and highwaymen; America's people would more accurately be called a manipulated lot. Howard Zinn has touched the revolutionary implication of this secret control: the American people are considered a potential enemy by their rulers. Why else would so much be kept secret, if not for fear that the American people might object if we knew what is being done in our name?

Certainly this totalitarianism will become more painful as it impinges on all our interests in the years ahead. The American empire will be seen as intolerably expensive. Our domestic welfare will become more of a shadow, the reality being oppression, not only for Third World people in America but for a majority of whites as well. Not just the material standard of living but the quality of services will deteriorate and the quality of work will become less and less meaningful. Brutal repression of resistance has already become routine, and less noticed but more sinister, the counter-insurgency technology and centralization of police power developed in Vietnam will be coming home for use against the American people. As a civilization our consensus on values will become more depleted as fewer people are able to identify with a "freedom" which in practice means competition, war, racism, machismo, and prisons. The pressure of revolutionary forces, as well as the irrelevance of old norms, will send us searching for new values and directions.

Our response to our history, as we discover it, should be neither to escape its implications nor to succumb to a useless guilt. It should be *shame* for whatever complicity we do share; *hate* for those who keep life-and-death decisions and ultimately our identities a secret from us; *solemn resolve* to end the "civilization" which kills us with lies as surely as it kills insurgency with force; *commitment* to opening ourselves to ancient values—solidarity, communalism, justice—whose time has come; and *thankfulness* to those whose suffering makes our redemption a possibility, both those who lead lives of resistance today and those "living souls," those swarms of "invisible dead," whose examples are alive in new hearts.

The Hopi Indians, who almost surely emigrated from Asia, have a legend which explains the problem well and suggests the solution. The Hopis believe that the universe originally was a seamless web of life, that the separations between people had resulted from migrations through various inevitable stages, but that all life will return eventually to its wholeness. The Hopis, like the Aztecs and Mayas, believed in a "lost" white people, represented by a figure named Pahána, which would be reunited with them in time. When the Spanish explorers came to the New World the Hopis naturally believed this was the return of Pahána, and welcomed them with sacred cornmeal and a hopeful spirit. The leader of the Hopi Bear Clan, in accord with prophecy, stepped forward to greet the Spaniard, extending his hand palm upward expecting the Pahána, as prophesied, to clasp his hand downward, the two hands forming the unity symbol, or Nakwach. Instead, the Spaniard thought the Hopi wanted a possession and commanded his officers to place some trinkets in the outstretched hand. The love of possession had blinded the settler to human solidarity.

The Vietnamese, Cambodians, and Laotian rebels of today say they believe in something like the return of Pahána. Their enemy, they say, is the American government, like the Spaniard who practices force and trinket-giving instead of peace. Their enemy is not the American people. They are not naïve about this; they know from cruel and concrete experience the degree to which people can be manipulated against their own best interests and humanity. But they call themselves a romantic people, too, not only referring to their own capacities but also to those of all people everywhere. They believe that people will rise up out of shame, out of indignities done to a universal system of values. I have seen factory administrators in North Vietnam, for instance, weep over the example of those Americans who have burned themselves in protest against the war, not because self-immolation was "correct" but simply because it goes beyond self-interest narrowly conceived and becomes an act of the human spirit; and, as a profoundly Buddhist act, it suggests the possibility that Americans can understand the suffering of Vietnam as the Vietnamese themselves do. The North Vietnamese study these and other acts of self-sacrifice to discover the lesson for themselves. These, as brave a people as exist in history, being moved by the protests of Americans: nothing better shows their ability to reach out in all directions, find the significance in everything, belittle nothing. They have a song, for example, about Norman Morrison, a Quaker who burned himself to death at the Pentagon in 1965, which contains these lines:

> *The flame which burned you will clear and lighten life,*
> *And many new generations of people will find the horizon,*
> *Then a day will come when the American people*
> *Will rise, one after another, for life.*

These perspectives will seem simply unbelievable to many Americans. Even some eastern European comrades of Vietnam were furious when they saw Hanoi widely publicize Morrison's death. These comrades believed it was a glorification of a useless gesture, and a misleading image of American protest possibilities. But the Vietnamese themselves were not mislead. While they themselves are highly organized and disciplined, they do not judge every action by narrow standards of effectiveness. They judge also by the spirit of an act and the qualities of the heart which are revealed. They believe that every sacrificial act in their history has helped to make them what they are, and should be memorialized for their children. In their experience they have seen people change: from slave mentality to a sense of self-determination, from oppressor to comrade of the oppressed. Theirs is an altogether different world view than that of the Anglo-Protestant and other colonizers. Their sense of karma stresses not the inevitability of sin, but the duty to endure suffering and seek a better world. They do not view themselves as a chosen few missionaries in the Heart of Darkness, but as selfless contributors to a people's war. Theirs is simply a version of the prophecy that the Paháná will come, extending a hand, without the gun or trinket, but instead with a desire to reunite humanity. The Vietnamese know the secret of the Pentagon Papers, the secret kept in corporate and military files. That secret is that the American people have a potential for revolution, for being free, if we ever recognize the truth of the unity which has been buried in our genocidal history. The prophecy is as ancient as the human subconscious; however, no one in Asia is waiting or depending on us to fulfill it and spare them their sacrifice. They have their own karma to fulfill in battle and construction. We are the only ones who can become the people we potentially are.

An Afterword on Election Year Strategy

It is vital for Indochina and America that Richard Nixon be forced into a complete withdrawal or face the loss of the Presidency in 1972. Since the clear likelihood is that Nixon will continue the war, we are faced with the necessity not of pressuring him but of bringing about his defeat.

His bombing and Vietnamization programs are evidence enough of his intent to stay in Indochina, but if we need more proof it will be found in his February, 1972, eight-point "peace plan." With this step Nixon has abandoned virtually any chance for a negotiated peace in 1972. His eight points continue the political tactic of seeming to stand for peace, in fact almost for the demands of the doves, while actually making preparations for intensified war.

Nixon seems to "set a date" for withdrawal, as demanded by the Vietnamese, but in fact only pledges a troop withdrawal six months *after* a settlement is negotiated: this is nothing new.

Nixon also seems to favor a political solution worked out among the Vietnamese themselves, with Thieu stepping down before elections, and with the NLF being permitted to take part in the process. But in fact he pledges a continued commitment to the Saigon regime, which means economic and military support indefinitely. The proposed elections in Saigon would be administered by the US–Thieu bureaucracy, whether Thieu stepped down or not. Such a process would be rigged from the start.

Nixon's authoritative February 9 foreign policy message goes further in spelling out the commitment to US control of South Vietnam through the Saigon administration. He praised "the overall picture of growing self-sufficiency and security in South Vietnam," claimed that 80 percent of the total population is "under effective government control," and called upon the NLF to "compete fairly in the political arena in South Vietnam." In short, he is asking the NLF to lay down their weapons in the face of the growing Saigon police force and trust to peaceful competition in elections designed by their mortal enemies. The NLF is to accept the legitimacy of the Saigon regime, with its American sponsorship, giving in on the very issue about which the war is being fought. This would mean nothing less than the surrender of the People's Revolutionary Government (PRG) in its claim to be a sovereign authority.

Many Americans may be confused because they do not understand that *neo-colonialism*—the indirect control and manipulation of South Vietnam by the US—is just as great an evil as US militarism. There is still a liberal image to "foreign aid" which makes a wide variety of Americans fail to realize its meaning as part of counter-insurgency. A real withdrawal by the US from Indochina would mean the stopping of all unilateral aid to Saigon, not simply the end of American pilots bombing and American GIs fighting the ground war. The demand for withdrawal must not stop with the issue of American forces; it must include the issues of neo-colonial economic aid and US-equipped mercenaries.

By continuing to insist on an American power position in South Vietnam, Nixon has really chosen to avoid negotiating except as a public relations device. This is apparent not only from his proposed negotiating terms but also from his bizarre act of unilaterally revealing the existence of secret talks between Kissinger and the Vietnamese. How can a plan rejected in secret in October, 1971, be accepted when it is unilaterally made public in February, 1972? How can negotiations be advanced if one side breaks the secret sessions with a denunciation of the other?

Nixon must have had other purposes in mind than a negotiated settlement in 1972. At least three separate purposes suggest themselves. First, to placate public opinion in an election year, which Kissinger himself admitted was a major motive in making the talks public. Besides trying to convince the public of his sincerity, Nixon apparently wants to continue the old tactic of smearing his Democratic enemies as pro-communist. Thus a great deal of emphasis was given in his revelation to the duping of Americans "into echoing [communist] propaganda." This theme later reached the preposterous level of Republican National Chairman Dole demanding that Senator Muskie withdraw his criticism of Nixon's proposal or withdraw from the race for the Presidency.

A second purpose, closely tied to the first, is to reduce the burden of Vietnam internationally as well as domestically. Nixon's foreign policy message claims with optimism that "Vietnam no longer distracts our attention from the fundamental issues of global diplomacy or diverts our energies from priorities at home." One case in point is Nixon's trip to China which he proudly believes has been accomplished without the US having to "give" anything in Indochina. This venture gives

Nixon an image of statesmanship which presumably will enhance his 1972 reelection possibilities. He probably hopes that the road to peace in Vietnam and to reelection in America travels through Peking and Moscow. He is sadly mistaken about the first, however, as the Vietnamese and Chinese have stated several times; and if his "peace effort" fails miserably, he may be sadly mistaken about his reelection plans.

But there is also a third purpose to Nixon's new negotiating face, if history is any precedent, and that is to prepare conditions for a future US escalation of the war. The "carrot-and-stick" policy has meant a squeeze of escalation followed by peace offers throughout both the Johnson and Nixon administrations. It will be difficult for Nixon to attempt escalation in an election year, but it is not out of the question if his diplomacy is frustrated.

If this escalation has not occurred before the election, it will surely come if Nixon is reelected. Unable to seek reelection in 1976, his whole term will be a "safe" one for Nixon to give play to his most reactionary impulses. In 1969 there was a sharp escalation in Vietnam as well as in repression of protest inside the US; in 1973, the same pattern should be expected. We have no parliamentary mechanism, like a vote of confidence, to prevent a minority President from committing us to even a nuclear war. That is one reason Nixon should be defeated at the polls.

But would a Democratic President be better than Nixon? From experience, the answer is no; as Nixon himself points out, this has been a Democrats' war all along. The stated position of the favored Democratic candidate, Senator Muskie, so far is better than Nixon in its stand on the bombing but contains the traditional contradictions which have always kept the US in Indochina. Muskie favors setting a date for the end of bombing and withdrawal of American military forces, but hesitates on the key question of Vietnamization, by urging

Saigon to seek "political accommodation" with its Vietnamese opponents (Muskie's official statement was made February 2, 1972). Does this mean cutting off military and economic aid to Saigon? What would happen if the Saigon government collapsed in chaos and a new government, with PRG-NLF membership, suddenly took its place? What about Laos, Cambodia, and Thailand? We are left uncertain by Muskie's position. Faced with a "communist takeover," not only in Saigon but in Laos and Cambodia with a hostile Republican opposition, with business confidence falling, with America's "image as a guarantor" threatened, there is no evidence that Muskie would simply withdraw. We do know that the Democrats traditionally have escalated to keep from losing, out of fear of repeating the 1951–52 experience when they were blamed for "losing" China and went down to defeat before Eisenhower, Nixon, and McCarthy. Would Muskie accept the responsibility of being called the "first President to lose a war"? There is nothing in his record to indicate he would.

Whether the Democrats realize it or not, however, this is not 1952. The man who accused the Democrats of "losing" China twenty years ago has now traveled there. The American people are not dominated by the politics of McCarthyism; the antiwar movements and other movements are larger today than at any time since the thirties. There is a climate of opinion which could protect a President who sincerely wanted to take the step of withdrawing from Indochina. The existence of this climate can only be made clear by the antiwar movement in this election year.

The war must be made an issue in 1972, reestablishing the domestic costs of escalation to the administration in power, proving once again that a President cannot be reelected again without ending US involvement in this war. We cannot allow Nixon a free hand to go on bombing Indochina for another four years: that might be another three million tons of bombs.

We should do no less in the short run than defeat Nixon and put as much pressure as possible on all other candidates. Thus the message would be not simply to Nixon, but to his opposition: that they will not find the support to defeat Nixon unless they take the strongest kind of position on the war. They will have to pledge:

(1) upon taking office, immediately to end all US bombing and ground and naval operations in North and South Vietnam, Cambodia, Laos, and Thailand by American military personnel, planes, and equipment;

(2) within a fixed period of time, such as three months, withdraw all remaining US personnel from Indochina;

(3) announce that all US economic and military aid to the repressive regimes of Indochina will be terminated within six months.

The case for taking a clear stand should draw on two lessons about negotiations from recent Vietnamese history. First, Pierre Mendes-France became prime minister of France in 1954 with a pledge that he would negotiate a settlement within one month or step down from office; he succeeded, with no political catastrophe to himself. Second, the Vietnamese should not be called upon to compromise, not only because they are in the right, but also because they have compromised several times in negotiations before, with bitter results. In 1946 at Fontainebleu they modified their demand for independence and agreed to "autonomy" within the French sphere of influence, only to be plunged back into war with France in less than one year. In 1954 at Geneva they came to the conference table direct from military victory at Dien Bien Phu, only to be forced to accept the compromise of temporary partition; with the betrayal of the pledge of 1956 elections, they were plunged again into a war situation. In the present phase of war, the NLF can be said to be fighting for "less" than they should. They stand for neutralism and a mixed economy rather than socialism;

for gradual rather than immediate steps toward reunification after the war, to cite two examples. But they cannot compromise on the fundamentals of national independence; that would be to compromise their basic existence. Promises of "free elections" mean nothing to them at this point, since they were promised the same opportunities in 1954 at Geneva. Only concrete deeds will ever convince them that the Americans are really leaving the destiny of Indochina to the Indochinese.

It is important to remind ourselves, in conclusion, that forcing the US government to withdraw from Indochina is a process which cannot be limited to electoral politics, though it might ultimately be reflected in ballots. It may be impossible to make any President, or presidential candidate (and those Wise Men of the ruling class he represents), see a "rational interest" in US withdrawal from Indochina. In the history of "respectable" dissent from the war, doves like Eugene McCarthy, Robert Kennedy, and Edmund Muskie have disagreed with the *conduct* of the war but not necessarily with the *goal* of American military and economic power in Southeast Asia. For that stake in power to disappear, all illusions about salvaging Vietnam would have to end. The American position would have to become *hopeless*. Then only through withdrawal could a self-interested ruling class even hope to regain influence in that region in the future (for example, through trade). The problem is that no candidate for the Presidency has acquiesced yet to that hopelessness. One way to imagine the war ending is not yet a real possibility. A new President—with a mandate to withdraw from both the voters and his establishment backers—could simply blame the war on "past mistakes" and, upon taking office, implement withdrawal (with agreements about POW releases, safety for America's former puppets, and multilateral aid worked out). This is a possibility in 1972 but not a likelihood, if we judge from either the history of the Democratic Party or the war itself.

Another scenario for ending the war would begin with a new and visible collapse of the Saigon Administration as US troops leave. The failure of Vietnamization would be reflected in battlefield defeats followed by NLF-ARVN accommodation, forcing Thieu to yield or be overthrown. At such a point, there would be powerful pressure for American escalation in the form of bombing, but perhaps even stronger international and domestic pressure *against* intervening. The American President, whether Nixon or Muskie in this case, recognizing at last the hopelessness of going on, could announce on television that Saigon had failed after America had done everything possible to save its ally, something like a doctor announcing the death of a patient after expensive and high-quality surgery.

This second scenario reminds us to keep presidential politics in a limited perspective: who the American President is will never be as important as the reality inside Vietnam itself. Much as incumbent officials claim that Hanoi is trying to win the war in the arena of American public opinion, this factor has always been secondary in significance to the battlefield in the minds of the Vietnamese. There was armed struggle in South Vietnam long before the first peace march in America. It was the frustration of American military action by the Vietnamese that caused the beginning of dialogue about Vietnam in America. If the Vietnamese resistance was weak, the Vietnamese themselves often say, even an American "dove" might invade; but if the resistance is strong enough, even a "hawk" can be made to withdraw.

While seeing this resistance as the primary determinant, however, we should never minimize the vital importance of public opinion in the historical struggle against the Vietnam war. The process of ending the war includes also the force of world public opinion, much of which has taken the side of the Indochinese people and nearly all of which has condemned and isolated the United States. The process began in America with a few isolated resisters, speakers, draft-card burners, and others, who were pictured as ineffectual, people who were willing to give up safe lives and act as free human beings, trusting their own force to end the war. But as the costs of the war mounted, and its immorality became more apparent, the resistance grew to massive proportions. The costs of the war, in blood and taxes, might have been acceptable as they were to the American people in World War II, were it not for the widespread protest which made the war seem of questionable value to the average American.

It was only at that point, in 1967–68, that politicians of either party began to react against the war, moving because of public opinion. Now we are a majority on this single issue: opposition to the war is almost universal, and resistance to it is supported or tolerated by millions of people. The only reason these vast numbers are silent is that they are confused. They believe the war may be ending, and when they are convinced it is not, they will act again. I believe Nixon is wrong in his judgment that Americans will tolerate a war like this one as long as their sons are spared. There are some Americans who care only about their sons, but there are many more who care about what becomes of their honor as a people when their government lies and kills so systematically.

The immediate task of those who care about Indochina is to clear up the confusion in American minds about the nature of this war which they are told is winding down. In a sense the antiwar movement is a victim of a certain success: most of its traditional demands have been met: stop the bombing of North Vietnam, negotiate with the NLF, withdraw American troops. What is left to expose and stop is the technological air war and the policy of neo-colonialism (Vietnamization). The exposure can come through many forms: demonstrations at the conventions of the two political parties, pressuring candidates at every level to take a stand, antiwar referendums, and other forms of "people's diplomacy" at city or state levels; continuing investigations of war crimes and the complicity of businesses, unions, churches, universities, and individuals in the war; support for political prisoners or exiles (which can build a climate encouraging to more Ellsbergs and Russos); and continued forms of resistance by everyone able to weaken the institutions carrying on the war; and the continued appearance of new radical consciousness and organization (which in itself is one of the more disturbing "cost factors" of the war in the view of US decision makers).

There is no single tactic, much less a personal act, which can end the Indochina war. The hope should instead be that each act, each heightening of consciousness, each organized protest, will have the effect of water dropping on stone, inevitably wearing the stone away. Each drop seems ineffective because its result on the stone is invisible; isolated drops will not have the effect of steady and ceaseless ones; no single drop will smash that stone. But in time the weak become strong and the strong weak; the water continues and the stone is no more.

March 1972

Sources

Responsibility for the formulations in this book are mine alone, but the original material was discovered and organized by other people. My particular thanks go to Fred Branfman, for his analysis of the air war, and to Bink Garrett, for his analysis of the "post-war" neo-colonial plans for staying in Vietnam. Small organizations such as Project Air War, Pacific News Service, and the Asian Information Group have performed great service by keeping a close watch on daily events in Indochina.

The specific source material used for this book is as follows, by topic:

The Pentagon Papers come in two editions, *The New York Times* Bantam paperback, and the four-volume set issued by Senator Gravel and Beacon Press. Background on Nixon and Kissinger, and quotes attributed to them, come from *The Kissinger-Nixon Doctrine* by Virginia Brodine and Mark Selden, to be published in 1972 by Harper & Row. Kissinger's major works cited in this book are: *Nuclear Weapons and Foreign Policy,* Harper & Row, 1957; *The Necessity for Choice,* Harper & Row, 1960; "The White Revolutionary: Reflections on Bismarck," in *Daedelus,* summer, 1968; *American Foreign Policy: Three Essays,* W. W. Norton, 1969.

Nixon's important statements on Vietnam, Japan, and China are in: "Asia After Vietnam," *Foreign Affairs* 46:24, October, 1967; "Why Not Negotiate in Vietnam," *Reader's Digest,* December, 1965; "Meeting the People of Asia," *Department of State Bulletin* 30:3, January 4, 1954; "State of the World" message, 1970, *Department of State Bulletin* 62:321, March 9, 1970; speech to American Society of Newspaper Editors, *The New York Times,* April 17, 1954; "Facing the Facts in Vietnam," speech to the Executives Club of New York, January 26, 1965, in *Vital Speeches of the Day,* March 15, 1965. The Nixon Doctrine, delivered in Guam, was reported in the July 26, 1969, *The New York Times,* not for direct quote.

On the Battlefield:
No Winding Down for Asians

Casualty figures for the US, ARVN, and "enemy" troops were obtained for 1961–71 from the South East Asia Division, Office of the Secretary of Defense for Public Affairs, December, 1971. The question of accommodation between the ARVN and NLF is discussed in Stephen Hosmer's "Viet Cong Repression and Its Implications for the Future," RAND/ARPA, May, 1970. North Vietnamese casualty estimates are provided by the Commission for the Investigation of US Imperialist War Crimes in Vietnam,

Hanoi, 1971. A thorough view of casualties, lack of medical care, prison torture, and total US ordnance expended can be found in several valuable US Senate hearings under the direction of Edward Kennedy and William Fulbright:

1. Senate Committee on Foreign Relations
   a. staff report on *Cambodia, May, 1970,* June 7, 1970
   b. staff report on *Laos, April, 1971,* August 3, 1971
   c. *Impact of the Vietnam War,* Congressional Research Service, Foreign Affairs Division, June 30, 1971

2. Senate Subcommittee on Refugees
   a. *Civilian Casualty, Social Welfare and Refugee Problems in South Vietnam,* Hearings, June 24–25, 1969
   b. *Refugee and Civilian War Casualty Problems in Laos and Cambodia,* Hearings, May 7, 1970
   c. *Refugee and Civilian War Casualty Problems in Indochina,* staff report, September 28, 1970
   d. *War-related Civilian Problems in Indochina, Parts I–II–III,* Hearings, April 21–22, 1971

Analysis of the 1971–72 ground offensives in Laos and Cambodia is from the *Bay Area Institute Newsletter,* January 13, 1972, from 9 Sutter St., San Francisco.

The Air War: Substituting Technology for American Troops

Most of the important research is developed by Project Air War, 1322 18th St. NW, Washington, D.C. 20036. North Vietnamese figures are from the war crimes report cited. The Senate Hearings, especially the June 30, 1970, Foreign Relations Committee staff report, are informative. Craterization and bulldozing effects are from the *Washington Post,* December 28, 1971. Chemical warfare is analysed in "Preliminary Report of the Herbicide Assessment Commission of the American Association for the Advancement of Science," published by the Kennedy subcommittee, April 21, 1971; "Ecological Effects of the War in Indochina," by G. H. Orians and E. W. Pfeiffer in *Science* 168: 544–554, 1970; "The

Destruction of Indochina," by the Stanford Biology Study Group, 1970; the "Leaf Abcission," by Ngo Vinh Long, 1970.

Sources on the electronic battlefield are *Investigation in Electronic Battlefield Program,* Hearings of the Senate Committee on Armed Services' Subcommittee on the Electronic Battlefield, November 18, 19, and 24, 1970; "The Death Harvesters," by Michael Malloy and "The Blind Bombers" by T. D. Allman, *Far Eastern Economic Review,* January 29, 1972; and the literature of NARMIC (National Action Research on the Military Industrial Complex), 160 North 15th St., Philadelphia, 19102.

The bombing of Laos is described in the August 3, 1971, staff report of the Foreign Relations Committee and the April 22, 1971, and May 7, 1970, refugee subcommittee hearings already cited; "The Wild Blue Yonder Over Laos," by Fred Branfman in *The Washington Monthly,* July, 1971; and "Laos: No Place to Hide," by Fred Branfman, Project Air War.

Civilian casualties are discussed in the refugee hearings already cited. The Government Accounting Office report on Cambodia is reported in *The New York Times* of December 5, 1971. My Lai, and the interview with Father Creswell, is discussed by Seymour Hersch in the January 22, 1972, *New Yorker.*

Forced Urbanization is outlined in "The Bases of Accommodation," by Samuel Huntington, *Foreign Affairs,* July, 1968. Also "Impact of Pacification on Insurgency in South Vietnam," by Robert Komer, RAND, August, 1970; and "War and Urbanization in Indochina," by Lawrence Moss and Zmarak Shalizi, in *Cambodia,* Washington Square Press, 1971.

Economic, Political, and Cultural Americanization

Most of the relevant reports are listed in the text of this book. The best summary article is "Aiding Pacification for Profit: US Postwar Development Plans for Vietnam," by Banning Garrett, November, 1971, available through Pacific News Service, 9 Sutter St., San Francisco. An earlier view is in "Mayday: the Case for Civil Disobedience," by Noam Chomsky in *The New York Review of Books,* June 17, 1971; also "The Asian Development Bank Wants to Integrate the Countries in Southeast Asia on the World Market," by Jacques Decornoy, *Le Monde,* February 9, 1971; "Oil and the War," by Malcolm Caldwell, *Liberation,* Spring, 1971; "Vietnam and the Pacific Rim Strategy," by Peter Wiley, *Leviathan,* June, 1969; *The Economics of Insurgency in the Mekong Delta of Vietnam,* by Robert Sansom, Massachusetts Institute of Technology, 1970; "The Economics of Central Vietnam," by V. L. Elliott, RAND, 1970; "US Cultural Neo-Colonialism: Arts and Literature in Saigon," an article supplied by Vietnamese students residing in the US.

The Truth Most Hidden

See *Vietnam, Inc.,* by Philip Jones Griffiths, Macmillan, 1971; *The Peasants of North Vietnam,* by Gerard Chaliand, Penguin, 1969; *Nguyen Du and Kieu,* by Foreign Language Publishing House, Hanoi, 1965; *Notes on the Cultural Life of the Democratic Republic of Vietnam,* by Peter Weiss, Dell, 1970; *We the Vietnamese,* edited by François Sully, Praeger, 1971; *The Other Side,* by Staughton Lynd and Tom Hayden, New American Library-Signet, 1966.

Why Vietnam? Ask, Why America?

A really radical and authoritative history of the US wars against the Indians does not exist. Some of the best material is in *Bury My Heart at Wounded Knee,* by Dee Brown, Holt, Rinehart and Winston, 1971; "The Winning of the West," by Richard Drinnon, available from him at Bucknell University, Lewisburg, Pa.; the 1881 classic *Century of Dishonor,* by Helen Hunt Jackson, Harper & Row, 1965; *To Serve the Devil,* edited by Paul Jacobs, Saul Landau, and Eve Pell, Vintage, 1971; *The Indian and the White Man,* edited by Wilcomb Washburn, Anchor, 1964.

One history recalls that this was a burning issue, *Was America a Mistake? An Eighteenth Century Controversy,* Commager and Giordanetti, Harper & Row, 1968.

Comparison of French and American religious-colonialist attitudes can be seen in "Hang Down Your Head Tom Dooley," by Robert Scheer, *Ramparts,* January, 1965; "The Vietnam Lobby," by Robert Scheer and Warren Hinckle, *Ramparts,* July, 1965, and *The French Presence in Cochinchina and Cambodia,* by Milton Osborne, Cornell, 1969.

Jung material is reprinted with the permission of Pantheon Books from *Memories, Dreams, and Reflections,* by C. G. Jung, © 1961, 1962, 1963 by Random House, Inc.

The Hopi mythology is described in *Book of the Hopi* by Frank Waters, Ballantine Books, 1969.